PELICAN BOOKS

THE
BLEAK AGE

(A171)

Owing to production difficulties it is impossible to maintain large stocks of our publications, and the titles available change so rapidly that the complete catalogue is of little value as a means of knowing what books are in print. If you are not already on our mailing list and would like to know when new books or reprints are added, please send in your name and address on a post card.

Suggestions for new additions are welcomed.

PELICAN BOOKS

THE BLEAK AGE

By

J. L. HAMMOND
Hon. D.Litt., Oxon

and BARBARA HAMMOND
Hon. D.Litt., Oxon

PUBLISHED BY

PENGUIN BOOKS

WEST DRAYTON MIDDLESEX ENGLAND
245 FIFTH AVENUE NEW YORK U.S.A.

First Published *1934*
Revised Edition first published in Pelican Books *1947*

MADE AND PRINTED IN GREAT BRITAIN
FOR PENGUIN BOOKS LTD., BY HAZELL, WATSON AND VINEY, LTD.
LONDON AND AYLESBURY

PREFACE

THE writers published in 1930, with the title *The Age of the Chartists,* a study of the social life of England in the thirties and forties of last century, giving special attention to the range and the character of the popular discontent that distinguished those years. In this little volume they have reconstructed and revised part of that book, in order to put into compact form the chapters that seemed to have a special bearing on our modern problem. For no problem to-day is more urgent than the problem that arises with the growth of leisure and the spread of common enjoyment. At first sight it may seem paradoxical to suggest that the way to examine the problems of an age of leisure is to study the experience of an age without leisure. Yet a little reflection will show that there is a vital connection between the two.

In the society described in the following pages the lot of the great mass of mankind was supposed to be the routine of eating, drinking, working, and sleeping. Leisure was the privilege of the few. The few therefore were educated to enjoy and use leisure; the mass of the population were educated for work, and for work that did not demand any considerable intelligence. Thus, for the general population, reason and feeling were left at the lowest level. Standards of taste and culture were in the keeping of a small class which had inherited, with leisure, the æsthetic and literary sensibilities that had been developed by generations accustomed to an atmosphere of ease and elegance. The Chartist movement, if the argument of this book is correct, was the revolt of the mass of the population against the bleak conditions to which this view of society reduced them. They refused to think of their own lives as nothing more than eating, drinking, working, and sleeping.

It is difficult to imagine a greater contrast than the contrast between that age and our own. Leisure is no longer the privilege of the few. The diversions of leisure are now enjoyed by all classes, for mass production, first used to supply man's needs, is now used to supply his pleasures. The columns of our newspapers, the scenes at a Test Match, the crowded cinemas, the radio talking, singing, or acting, in every street, these, the chief phenomena of our social life, will give to posterity the impression of a society with universal leisure, depending no longer on the taste or judgment of the few for its guidance, but using universal suffrage in its manners as in its politics, in the choice of its culture as in the choice of its Parliaments. Of the revolutions that have followed the war this may prove to be the most important.

The importance of this change has not received the attention it deserves. Rostovtzeff, the social historian of the Roman Empire, discussing the decay that set in in the third century, asks a disconcerting question: "Is not every civilization bound to decay as soon as it begins to penetrate the masses?" His conclusion will seem unnecessarily gloomy to most people, but his question serves a useful purpose in reminding us that the new conditions under which we live offer a challenge to our civilization. The inventions that spread leisure have been followed by the inventions that provide everybody with ways of using that leisure. It has often been said of the steam-engine that it came into the world before the world was ready for it. Future ages may make the same comment on the cinema and the radio. For, if they bring unprecedented opportunities for educating reason and feeling, they bring unprecedented opportunities for corrupting them. Of these inventions it is even truer than it was of the others, that their best use demands the intelligent co-operation of the entire community. In the long run the test of our civilization will be its success in producing a society that can choose between the good use of these inventions and the bad.

Our chief danger comes from the tradition described in this little volume. For though we have abandoned the view that only a small class should have leisure, we have not abandoned the implications that belonged to it. We have not yet realized that our experiment—an experiment new to history in respect of its scale—can only succeed if we educate all classes for leisure. It is absurd to expect from a raw mass of untrained mind and emotion, submitted to the influences of the cinema and the radio, an educated taste. The educated man can respond to the stimulus of ideas or the beauty of art; the uneducated man responds to effects that are sensational, immediate, astonishing, and crude. And as the provision of amusement is governed largely, though fortunately not wholly, by commercial motives, the taste of the uneducated man is more likely to be satisfied than the more exacting taste of the educated. The first effect of the cinema has been the depression of the theatre just when serious drama had made a remarkable recovery after a century's eclipse. It is difficult to imagine the plays of Euripides succeeding in a society where the entertainment of the theatre was organized and produced by profit-making companies, for a society to whom leisure was a new experience.

All this is so plain that the reader may retort that he need not study the time of the Chartists to appreciate its truth. Unfortunately we have not yet taken this truth so seriously as to act upon it. We depend for the discrimination between the good and the bad in our theatre, our cinema, our literature, our press, on the judgment of a society that is still brought up on the plan that was in force when the mass of men and women were supposed to have nothing to do with culture. It is true that we spend large sums on popular education, and that we provide large facilities for taking intelligent boys from the poorest home to the University. But it is also true that though everybody votes at twenty-one and though most people begin to influence public taste long before twenty-one, most boys and girls have no education after fourteen. Yet there is surely no time when education is more needed. For most purposes this population is an adult population; it has passed into the world of industry; it has a new sense of independence; it reads the newspapers; goes to the cinema; listens to the wireless; chooses between one pleasure and another; between a pleasure that merely excites and a pleasure that enlarges the mind. In this critical time when it is interpreting a new world, when its mind and taste are being formed by all the influences to which it is subject, when, owing to the perfection of our machines, it has adult habits without adult tasks, it is deprived of all the education that the class educated for leisure receives from literature or history, and is told to trust to the school of life, a school in which, as beauty and peace are steadily destroyed, few of its scholars can hope to learn the wisdom that nature has taught mankind. Nearly twenty years ago Mr. Fisher provided a plan to meet this urgent need. The need was urgent then; it is still more urgent now. Yet we are told that we cannot afford such a plan. This is only another way of saying that we think that a society can use leisure without being educated for it.

The challenge that is offered to us is offered of course to other societies of our time. But there is one respect in which we are trying to do something more ambitious than certain of our neighbours. In every society there is a mass mind that can be interested and excited by ideas and emotions. In the Chartist time England left this mind alone, giving scarcely any education and trusting to its police to prevent any dangerous outburst. In certain States to-day, Russia, Germany, Italy, a deliberate attempt is made to take this primitive force and to direct and control it, as the rulers of the State wish, making it a defence for a particular type of government. If we wanted to describe the ideal of our democracy, we should say that it attempts so to educate its citizens as to give them independent qualities of intelligence and temper, seeking a unity that is not merely the unity of the closed mind. It is a noble aim, but how do we set about it? We set about it as if we were still in the state of mind of the rulers of the age of the Chartists. For we treat as if they were still merely the servants of profit-making industry the mass of boys and girls between fourteen and eighteen who are to be the guardians of our culture.

HEMEL HEMPSTED,
August 1934.

IN this edition, which is nearly twice as long as the earlier edition of *The Bleak Age*, new material has been inserted, more chapters from *The Age of the Chartists* have been incorporated, and the book has been re-arranged and in part rewritten.

HEMEL HEMPSTED,
April, 1947.

CONTENTS

THE BLEAK AGE

CHAPTER I

INTRODUCTORY

DISCONTENT

IF anyone were asked to give the causes of the Gordon Riots he would not hesitate long about his answer. He might turn to the pages of *Barnaby Rudge* for a graphic picture of the nightmares that religious terror could excite in an ignorant and credulous populace. He might quote the letter in which Burke, who had risked his life in the riots, appealed to the Government to be moderate in the hour of punishment, on the ground that the guilt of the rioters was shared by the nation, since the law till lately had lent its sanction to intolerance, and the heads of the Church and Dissenting communities had wilfully encouraged it. He might describe the scene in a street in Newgate where a chimney-sweeper held a Bible upside down as he pretended to read it, while a mob searched the house of a trembling merchant. He would point to the weakness of a discredited Government, to the negligence of the City magistrates, to the want of a police force, in order to explain how lawlessness gained the upper hand and London fell for some days into the wild power of rage and plunder.

> "When the rude rabble's watchword was 'destroy'
> And blazing London seem'd a second Troy."

If the same person were asked to give the causes of the Chartist movement, he would be much less ready with an explanation. For he would see at once that no such simple analysis would account for the facts; that this agitation was connected with others, each of them significant of active and conscious discontent; that

violence, the most important fact in the Gordon Riots,
was the least important fact in the Chartist demonstra-
tions; that unlike the mob, drawn by a strong passion
which spent its inarticulate fury in burning Newgate
prison to the ground, the men and women who kept the
Chartist movement alive had a steady and responsible
quarrel with the conditions of their lives, which gave a
unity to efforts that look distracted and confused. The
London mob shouting for Wilkes, for Gordon, for Queen
Caroline, obeyed a simple emotion; the silent crowds
tramping to Newcastle Moor or leaving the factories of
Bradford or Halifax to climb the overlooking hills for a
Chartist meeting, obeyed a deeper and more complex
sense of wrong.

There was a good deal of lawlessness in eighteenth-
century England; particular grievances, like Enclosure
Bills, or dear food, or new machines, excited riots in one
place or another. This kind of violence continued in the
next century: the riots against the raising of prices for
the Covent Garden Theatre lasted several days, and succeeded in their object; there were savage attacks on
the Irish quarter in more than one northern town; in
1816 mobs were moving about in East Anglia with
banners inscribed "Bread or blood"; the enclosure of
Otmoor provoked small farmers and labourers to a kind
of guerrilla struggle. But anyone who throws his mind
over the succession of popular movements on a larger
and less local scale in the nineteenth century will see that
working-class discontent assumed in that century a more
serious character and significance. The Luddite rising in
the Midlands and the North in 1811 and 1812; the
agrarian revolt in the southern counties in 1830; the
passionate movement inspired by Owen which collected
the energy and enthusiasm of the working classes
throughout England for a great constructive idea in
1833; the Chartist agitation, in its several forms in the
thirties and forties—all these are expressions of a spirit
of which there is little trace in eighteenth-century Eng-

land: the resentment of men convinced that there is something false and degrading in the arrangement and the justice of their world.

When this discontent appeared, sensible and public-spirited writers pointed out to the poor that they were much better off than their fathers and grandfathers. Invention had made commodities cheaper, food and clothing were more abundant; the mills increased family incomes; the poorest people wore stockings; and in other respects the humblest person enjoyed advantages that had been out of the reach of the lords and squires of other ages. These contentions have been repeated by recent writers who think that historians have been apt to draw the life of this time in colours too sombre for the truth. Statisticians tell us that when they have put in order such data as they can find, they are satisfied that earnings increased and that most men and women were less poor when this discontent was loud and active than they were when the eighteenth century was beginning to grow old in a silence like that of autumn. The evidence, of course, is scanty, and its interpretation not too simple, but this general view is probably more or less correct. If, then, there is for the first time systematic and widespread discontent, the explanation must be sought outside the sphere of strictly economic conditions. The rebels, though they included men and women who found it difficult to keep the wolf from the door, were not composed altogether of starving handloom weavers, or unemployed mill-workers. There were other elements in the anger and the envy of the times, and to understand what those elements were it is necessary to look a little more closely into the character of this new society and the general colour of its life.

It is obvious that when men are wandering over the steppes in search of food their pursuits and interests are too narrow in range to make the term "civilization" suitable to describe their manner of life. Civilization implies some degree of independence; it implies that man has

learnt how to mould his surroundings to his own purposes; that he is not in complete subjection to nature or
even just holding his own in a stern struggle. If, then,
we are comparing the life of Manchester with the life of
the steppes or the tropical forest, we think chiefly of this
difference in material power. That is the distinguish-
ing difference. But when we compare two ages or two
societies, both of them in a later stage of development,
both of them able to follow a settled life and to express
their character, their tastes, and ideas in complicated
and deliberate institutions, we do not merely compare
their material circumstances. If we compare Western
civilization with that of China, or the civilization of
modern Lancashire with that of Rome under Augustus,
we do not merely count the material advantages that
one possesses and the other lacks—railways, cotton
mills, a stock exchange, other signs and products of
economic wealth. We survey the whole of their social
life, their religion, their art, their literature, their
methods of government and justice, the several institutions in which their public life finds form and expression, the relationships and the sentiments of classes to
each other. We recognize, that is, that such a society has
to satisfy a wider range of needs than the needs that the
nomad is trying to satisfy on the steppes or the tropical
man in the depths of the forest. To understand discontent we must keep this range in mind.

For discontent comes from the imagination. "Human
sorrow springeth of man's thought." Poverty may produce such a state of the imagination; injustice may produce it; inequality may produce it; but we may find
a society enduring great poverty, suffering what seems
to us gross injustice, living under conditions so unequal
as to look as if they were deliberately designed to pro-
voke envy, in which discontent is unknown. We know
that some men like St. Francis find happiness in poverty
just because their imagination finds in renunciation and
hardship a field for the sublime in thought and action.

Bridges describes such natures in the *Testament of Beauty* .

> "And mystic Vision may so wholly absorb a man
> that he wil loathe ev'n pleasure, mortifying the flesh
> by disciplin of discomfort so to strengthen his faith.
> Thus tho' 'twas otherwise than on Plato's ladder
> that Francis climb'd—rather his gentle soul had learn'd
> from taste of vanity and by malease of the flesh—
> he abjured as worthless ev'n what good men will call good."

To thinkers who held, as most Radicals held a century ago, that justice demanded that every adult man should have a vote for Parliament and that any other political arrangement was vicious, it seemed difficult to believe that social life had been happy or successful when government had been despotism, despotism it may be with a kind face, but still despotism. Yet as we look back over history we see that almost every sort of government has been made tolerable to human nature, and that men and women have lived with equanimity under political systems which left them not merely without political rights, but without any pretence of personal liberty. In such cases it is clear that in some way or by some device these excluded men and women were given the sense of sharing in the life of this society; their imagination and their emotions were satisfied, some would say deceived, by its dispositions or its illusions. For if men and women are to be attached to a society, they must look on it as something in which they have a part; a world in which what we may call the common mind finds in some degree, or by some means, scope, peace, comfort, and self-respect; in which distinctions of class and fortune, however hardly and sternly drawn, do not forbid all ties of sympathy, all unity of sentiment.

Professor Graham Wallas, describing the difference between the reactions produced by human and .non-human obstruction to our impulses, points out that when Shakespeare sets out the ills that drive men to suicide he gives

"The oppressor's wrong, the proud man's contumely,
The pangs of despised love, the law's delay,
The insolence of office, and the spurs
That patient merit of the unworthy takes"

and does not mention the want of food and clothing
from which he must himself have suffered during his
first wanderings from Stratford. So Wordsworth draws a
poor man holding dispute

"With his own mind, unable to subdue
Impatience through inaptness to perceive
General distress in his particular lot;
Or cherishing resentment, or in vain
Struggling against it; with a soul perplexed,
And finding in herself no steady power
To draw the line of comfort that divides
Calamity, the chastisement of Heaven,
From the injustice of our brother man."

Neither Shakespeare nor Wordsworth would have
doubted that a man might be less poor and less uncomfortable than his grandfather, and yet have in his con-
sciousness a more wounding sense of balked instincts,
more of the sting of defeat, more of that impatience of
calamity which springs from a belief that it is injustice.
It is the aim of these pages to inquire what it was in the
conditions and setting of English social life in the first
half of the nineteenth century that created this sense of
wrong.

CHAPTER II

THE REMEDY OF THE ANCIENT WORLD

COMMON ENJOYMENT

THE art of government may be described in one aspect as the art of making men and women think that the world they inhabit obeys in some degree their own ideas of justice. Cavour's often-quoted saying that anyone can govern in a state of siege meant, of course, that when you are released from this task and government becomes naked force, statesmanship, a rare quality, ceases to be needed, and firmness, which is more common, takes its place. Peoples, great and small, have often been ruled against their will by firmness. But clearly, if we wish to understand the discontent of the nineteenth century, we shall learn less from ages and places where government was of this character than from those in which rulers sought to justify their authority, and societies sought to satisfy their self-respect. Bacon pointed out that when Virgil attributed to Augustus the best of human honours, he made this the mark of his rule, describing him as "a conqueror giving laws to consenting peoples." Bacon used this to illustrate his argument that "it was ever holden that honours in free monarchies and common-wealths had a sweetness more than in tyrannies, because the commandment extendeth more over the wills of men, and not only over their deeds and services." It may help us to understand the discontent of Manchester amid all the improvements and new knowledge that the Industrial Revolution brought, if we ask ourselves in what sense Virgil's boast was true, and what there was in Roman civilization which gave it the appearance of a voluntary or consenting society.

As we look back over the history of Graeco-Roman civilization we find every variety of political government, but through all those varieties we see that a definite effort was made to command the wills of men, and not merely their deeds and services. Elaborate care was taken to produce a stable society creating a sense of fellowship, by satisfying the imagination of the ruled, whether their political rights were considerable or insignificant. And as that civilization reflects the experience of the most capable peoples in Europe, whose society endured over a long space of time, it is worth while to consider what methods were used to make men and women think that the world in which they lived obeyed their own ideas of justice.

On this aspect of ancient history we have learnt a great deal in recent years from the discovery and interpretation of inscriptions. We see that what was most important in the civilization of classical Greece or the Hellenized East, or the Roman Empire, was the quality of its city life; the character of the institutions and customs which inspired, or sought to inspire, a common pride and common emotion in populations tempted into strife by savage inequalities of fortune and sharp antipathies of history and race. To appreciate the importance of those institutions it is necessary to remember what difficulties these societies had to overcome.

The struggles of rich and poor in ancient Greece, of city and city, were bitter and incessant. Greek literature is full of this strife; the fear of revolution is constant; Isocrates said that the Greeks feared their fellow citizens more than they feared a foreign enemy. The reason is partly that the Greeks were intelligent and contentious above their neighbours, pursuing ambitions greater and nobler (it has been said by Dr. Bevan that their great achievement was bringing freedom and civilization into union), partly that they lived in an atmosphere of fierce economic competition, and trade routes and commercial openings had an exceptional importance for peoples whose livelihood depended upon them.

It is not surprising, then, that Greek history is full of strife, and that it seems to end in political failure. Yet the history of the world has been largely moulded by the achievements of this small and distracted people: the new spirit they brought into politics; the beauty of art, life, and manners, that fascinated first Macedon, then Rome; the literature and science that made them the teachers of Europe until the Roman Empire was lost in the Dark Ages, and again so soon as the Renaissance summoned the ghost of Greece from libraries and monasteries, where it had slept through the storm. A people apparently given up to war and conflict left these riches to mankind. What is the explanation? It is to be found in the power of disinterested emotion to lighten the dark misery that man suffers when shut up within the narrow circle of selfish aims and cares. The class struggle was veiled or softened by the moral influence of common possessions, the practice of social fellowship was stimulated by the spectacle of beautiful buildings, and the common enjoyment of the arts and culture of the time. If the many and the few, the rich and poor, had pursued their quarrels in a world untouched by this gentle and mysterious spirit, a State like Athens could not have lived long enough to lay her spell upon the world.

When we turn to the history of the East under Alexander's successors, we come on perpetual wars in which brothers contend with brothers and every king has a rival of his own blood, so that these rulers, proud as they were of their civilized traditions, seem to differ little in fact from the oriental despots whose culture they despised. Of the poverty and hardships of life among their subjects, scholars like Dr. Tarn draw a melancholy picture. Yet we find in the midst of all this strife of class, and of fratricidal war between rivals for Alexander's empire, a brilliant city life, where the arts flourish and beauty and grace are admired. The Seleucid kings made deliberate efforts to foster and develop that life as the means to progress and unity, as an educating influence over the indigenous races brought into contact with Greek ideas. The saying that Arrian put into the mouth of Alexander (quoted by J. S. Reid in *The Municipalities of the Roman Empire*) is significant: "My father led you down from the mountains to the plains, when you lived in scattered places he made you dwellers in cities, and he equipped you with institutions adapted to your changed mode of life." The last sentence sums up the task of a developing civilization, and it has a special importance in the history of the people who first made town-planning an art.

The Roman Empire established long spells of peace over a great part of the world, succeeding in this respect where Greece and the Hellenized East had failed. The Romans gained their Empire by their military prowess and their political genius, but for the purposes of this comparison military success is the least important fact about their Empire. It was not on that ground that St. Augustine, in *De Civitate Dei*, bade the citizens of the City of God look to Rome for inspiration. The secret of its power was its ability to satisfy and attach the races and classes that had come under its rule. The world in which this success was achieved was a world that had been thrown into disorder by a century of strife and exploitation. War and conquest had brought opportunities of acquisition and profit that had produced the great slave plantations, the plunder of the provinces, the terrible slave wars, and the civil strife in which great war lords had nearly extinguished Roman civilization in their struggles for power. In this war the Roman Empire had succeeded in controlling and composing the rivalries of men, races, and classes by creating a new order, inspired by the Greek tradition aided, as we can see from Tarn's pages, by the Hellenistic religions that flourished and expanded when the Greek genius had ceased to express itself in great literature. For the municipal civilization that spread over the Empire brought back the amenities and the sympathies on which a Greek community relied. We know from such books as those of Dill, Reid, and Rostovtzeff how various an enjoyment of life was organized in the cities of the Empire; how great an importance was given to public beauty, how lavishly the rich, and even the middle classes, spent their money on theatres, baths, libraries, and temples; how widely, as Greenidge put it, the supply to the poor of what we call luxuries was deemed an obligation of wealth. The basis of this social life was the tradition of the Greek city, with its habits of common enjoyment, and its fostering of a common culture.

How persistent was this tradition, even though the rulers of the State might differ as sharply as Augustus differed from Pericles, or the spirit of politics as sharply as that of fifth-century Athens from that of the Antonines, we can see when we remind ourselves that a man visiting Athens in the fifth century B.C., Rhodes in the second century B.C., and a Roman town in Africa or Spain in the second century A.D. would have noted that certain characteristics were common to all of them. First he would see that public beauty held a sovereign place in the ambitions and esteem of the time. The boast made by Smyrna when she claimed the title of "First City of Asia by beauty and importance, most brilliant and glory of Ionia," named the distinctions that every city, Greek, Hellenist, or Graeco-Roman, put first. The beauty of which cities were proud was not beauty hidden away in private houses, but beauty that the whole world could see and admire. An observation by a Greek sophist, Archytas of Tarentum, which Cicero quotes in his treatise on Friendship, throws some light on their feeling about it: "If a man should climb alone into heaven and look upon the structure of the world and the beauty of the stars, he would find no pleasure in

that spectacle though it would fill him with delight if he
had someone to whom he could speak of it." A hungry
man coming on food in a desert island would not say
that he could not enjoy that food because he was alone;
Robinson Crusoe was glad enough to eat before he had
the company of Friday. The sophist held, then, that the
enjoyment of beauty is not, like the enjoyment of food,
an individual satisfaction; that it is connected in some
way with man's social nature. He held, that is, with
some modern philosophers, that beauty is a reality
which is perceived specially in the contact between
minds. It was perhaps this conviction or this intuition
that led the Greeks to realize the power that beauty has
over men's sympathies and imagination, and in consequence to look upon beauty as essentially for common
enjoyment. Demosthenes reminded the Athens of his
days that Themistocles or Aristides lived in plain houses
indistinguishable from those of their neighbours, and
that the great buildings were to be found in the Acro-
polis. Alcibiades outraged public sentiment by painting
his house. The Greeks then regarded beauty as a spiritual
power that could influence politics, helping to make men
generous and public-spirited, able to forget in a common
loyalty the passions that tended to drive them and keep
them apart. "Even a man whose soul is utterly
burdened," said Dion Chrysostom of Pheidias' statue
of Zeus at Olympia, "who has drained in his life
the cup of sorrow and misfortune and has not closed
his eyes in sleep, will forget, when he stands opposite
this statue, all the terrors and hardships of human life."

The second thing that such a visitor would have
noticed was the great proportion of expenditure in
wealth and labour that was devoted to things that were
for common enjoyment. This was illustrated not only
by the beauty and grace of the public buildings, but also
by the amenities that were brought within the reach of
poor people. Every town had its theatres, its baths, its
public games and festivals, its great gardens and colon-

nades. Many towns engaged public doctors, and sophists, philosophers, and grammarians were generally relieved of all public burdens. All this elaborate provision for the amusement of the mass of the population was made possible by the possession of common land and other common property, and partly by the fashion of private liberality for public objects. One of the first uses to which a rich man thought of putting his wealth was to adorn his city or to make an endowment that would associate his name and memory with its renown and the happiness and gratitude of its citizens; he would build a theatre or racecourse, or he would set aside a sum of money for education or for providing baths for the poor or for the slaves. He believed with Bacon that "riches are for spending and spending for honour and good actions."

This truth is illustrated in the sermon on Poverty which Lucian put in the form of a dialogue between the cobbler and the cock inhabited by the soul of Pythagoras. Certain reflections are common to all the arguments by which philosophers and teachers have sought at different ages to persuade the poor that they are happier than the rich. All touch on the pleasures or comforts of the body. Horace says that a rich man cannot hold more in his stomach than a poor man; Lucian contrasts the afflictions of the rich, gout, pneumonia, and other diseases due to intemperance, with the good health of the poor, who live on sprats and a bunch of onions; Paley reminds the poor man that if anything unusual comes his way he finds a feast, whereas the epicure dines too well every day to enjoy any novelty. At all ages again philosophers have dwelt on the cares and responsibilities of the rich and powerful. "You sleep well on a rug," said Martial to the slave, "your master lies awake on a bed of down." Lucian told the poor in a lively passage that the rich have to risk their lives in the field as commanders of horse or foot, "whereas you with but a wicker shield have little to carry and nothing

to impede your flight, and are ready to celebrate the
victory when the general offers sacrifice after winning
the battle." Paley argues that the poor escaped the
anxieties of the rich about their children. "All the provision which a poor man's child needs is contained in
two words, industry and innocence." These arguments
are used to console the poor in all ages. But we notice
one important difference: whereas in the nineteenth
century the argument runs that there is no capital without the rich, no production without capital, and no
wages without production, Lucian puts it that the rich
had to toil that the poor might have baths, shows, and
everything else, to their hearts' content. That is, whereas
the modern economist put it that the poor man is indebted to the rich for his livelihood, the ancient moralist
said he was indebted to the rich for his luxuries.

The third feature of public life that such an observer
would notice was the great part played in social life by
voluntary associations. This was specially noticeable
in the Roman Empire, where all classes were encouraged to form clubs and colleges, for the maintenance
of their corporate dignity, the celebration of a patron
or festival, or the organization of common pleasure or
thrift, or to secure for the poorest and humblest person
such a funeral as would not leave him an outcast in
death. If the highest class had its group in the Curiales,
and the men who rose to wealth from the freedman
class had their group in the Augustales, the lower classes
of freedmen, artisans, and slaves marched under their
own flags in great processions to their special places at
the games, and kept festivals and ceremonies at which,
if only for an hour, the common life of the city seemed
more important than all the inequalities of fortune. We
know from the works of Dill and R. H. Barrow that
in such a group a slave would sometimes preside over
freedmen.

But the observer would notice on his travels through
time and space a fourth feature. He would be struck

by a terrible decline in the standard of pleasure, and the character of the enjoyment provided for the city populations. He would see that, though the Roman Empire had solved a problem that had defeated the Greeks, the problem of creating a large political unit in which peace and order prevailed, it had allowed the culture of the Greeks to degenerate into brutal and savage entertainment. This, indeed, is part of the explanation of the fall of the Roman Empire. For the Roman Empire, as a civilizing organization, depended on its power to satisfy the social imagination of its subjects, and to mould raw races in the Roman pattern. Montesquieu said that the Romans received slaves from all parts of the world and returned them as Romans. This is, of course, a picturesque exaggeration, but the phrase describes the Roman genius at its best, the spirit that distinguishes and explains its success. Tolerance and assimilation were the secrets of its power. The history of the Empire is the history, in one sense, of an euthanasia, the decay of that civilizing and assimilating power of which municipal life had been the most striking expression. Pelham said that its animated city life was a substitute for politics, and that Rome was thus reconciled to the loss of her republican liberties. But there came a time when the virtue had gone out of that life, when the Roman system had lost its ability to mould and assimilate new and raw material, when its peasant population had been depressed or ousted by slave labour, when its city crowds were no longer composed of independent and self-respecting artisans, but of loungers who lived for low pleasure, when its legions were filled by men with no Roman tradition and no Roman discipline. Diocletian's reorganization of the Empire at the end of the second century A.D. marks the formal recognition of these facts. Bureaucracy became omnipotent; the cities lost their self-government; the needs of the State were met by compulsory services based on a caste system, and the Empire sought to satisfy the social imagination of its subjects by the pomp of its ceremonies and the sheer magnificence of its rulers.

The decline of the Roman Empire was due to a number of causes, but in accounting for it we must give some importance to the contrast between the Greek audience listening the livelong day to the plays of the great dramatists, and the mob in Rome, representing, as it was bitterly said, the dregs of the human race, watching in uproarious excitement, or in savage suspense, the combats of the gladiators and the slaughter of wild beasts. The gladiatorial games began as private funeral shows, borrowed from the customs of the Etruscans, but ambitious men soon saw the use to which they might be put. In the last century of the Republic they became State shows, and under the Empire they grew steadily in importance. The first stone amphitheatre was built in 29 A.D. by a friend of Augustus. The atmosphere of the amphitheatre corrupted or destroyed dramatic art in Rome. De Quincey put it that the Roman drama was killed prematurely by the bloody realities of the amphitheatre, as candlelight by daylight. Whereas in Athens it was held to be wrong to let Medea be presented killing her children on the stage, in Rome the mob demanded that live men should be put to death when a death scene came into a play. The best men and the best rulers sought to divert public taste from these scenes of cruelty by introducing Greek games and shows, but they had very limited success. The later Emperors, knowing that city life had been a civilizing force in the history of Greece and Rome, sought to combat the dangers that threatened and finally extinguished the Roman Empire, by creating new cities, hoping thus to tame their fierce neighbours. But a city culture that had degenerated into the debauching of taste could not turn barbarous races into Romans, for it could not preserve the Romans themselves from their barbarous passions.

No attempt has been made in these few pages to

estimate the happiness and misery of the poor under Greek or Roman government; to calculate how far social amenities compensated for the privations and the cruelties to which they were exposed; to consider all the evils that a society suffers and inflicts if its basis is slavery; to trace the causes, so brilliantly discussed in the third volume of Toynbee's Study of History, of the fate that overtook "a thousand city-states, living side by side, in peace and concord." That is a task for scholars. The aim of this survey is different and more modest. It is to see what light we can draw from well-known facts about ancient history for our inquiry into the causes of social discontent in the nineteenth century. In the history of Graeco-Roman civilization we are watching the government, not of docile or acquiescent races, or of primitive and unsophisticated tribes, but of societies conspicuously intelligent, critical, and high-spirited. Or we may put it that we are watching experiments in group life which have a special value for all time, because we possess rich and illuminating records of the active and interesting peoples that were engaged in making them, and a literature in which those experiments are discussed, explained, and criticized, by acute and penetrating minds. In such a world the problem of making a stable society is not a problem set to force, but a problem set to wisdom; it is not an essay in terrorism, but an essay in statesmanship. The same problem was set to nineteenth-century England, for the English people were no more docile and acquiescent than the communities for whose satisfaction this elaborate city life was devised. And the Industrial Revolution, which had spread far and wide the improvements that economists describe, had put to that statesmanship problems not less subtle and difficult than the problems put to Augustus or the Antonines in the government of a Roman province.

CHAPTER III

THE NEW PROBLEM

THERE have been long ages in the history of the world when social life has been languid and impoverished, and yet there has been no revolt of which literature gives any record. Custom will reconcile men and women to conditions that they would find intolerable if they came fresh to them. For custom has a magic that takes the sting out of injustice, making it seem rather the decree of heaven than the sin of man. Thus the spell that custom casts on the imagination is the greatest conservative force in the world, a force so strong that it will keep life in institutions which have long ceased to serve, or even to remember, the purpose that brought them into use. As life follows its circle of unbroken routine no fierce questions are asked about facts and conditions that seem part of everyday experience, the face of a familiar world. When, therefore, society is passing through changes that destroy the life of custom, the statesman who seeks, in Bacon's words, to command man's will and not merely his deeds and services has a specially difficult task, for those changes bring into men's minds the dreaded questions that have been sleeping beneath the surface of habit.

England at this time was passing through such changes. Some critics argue that the Industrial Revolution described by Toynbee has been pushed into a false importance. It is true that that revolution was a phase in a series of changes reaching far back into history. Some may put the beginning of the revolution on the day when Columbus set sail in his cockle shell to cross the Atlantic; others when Godfrey de Bouillon led crusaders and merchants to the Holy Land, bringing the West with its needs and energy once more into touch

with the resources of the East; others will go back to
the time when Cretan and Phoenician first learned how
rich a basin holds the Mediterranean Sea. The student
may take his choice. But whatever the date and whatever the cradle we name for this great event, it remains
true that the England of this time was an England in
movement, that speculation was in the air, that the
indolent influence of habit was shaken, and that the
statesman could no longer hope that half his work would
be done for him by custom.

Another aspect of this age must be kept in mind. It
was an age of energy and power, in which man eclipsed,
in his new authority over nature, the spectacular
triumphs of the architects and engineers of Rome. We
can dig up to-day the bones of strong cities, which had
once a vigorous and brilliant life in the waste of the
African desert, desert when the Romans went there,
desert to-day. Those buried columns speak of a miracle,
but of a miracle less astonishing than the creation of the
railway power that conquered distance, the obstacle that
had so long arrested the development of Europe; less
astonishing than the creation of the Lancashire cotton
industry, its raw material brought across the Atlantic
Ocean, its finished products carried round the Cape to
India and the China Seas. There was no question here
of a society drawing its ebbing breath under some stroke
of disease or destiny. Man's power stared the new
world in the face. In such an age the inequalities of
life are apt to look less like calamities from the hand
of heaven and more like injustices from the hand of
man.

Upon the society in whose manner of life and sense of
power this change was taking place, there had fallen the
shock of the French Revolution. We can measure the
effect of that shock if we compare the world of ideas
within which Wordsworth or Coleridge or Southey or
Mill were moving when they reflected on the future of
society, with that in which Gibbon was moving when he

asked himself in a famous passage whether the civilized
world might ever suffer again a calamity like the fall of
the Western Empire. The dangers and the dreams that
haunt the nineteenth-century thinkers never appear on
his horizon. He looks out from a world composed and
untroubled about its basis; they belonged to a world
where the moral foundations of society, and the justice
and the power of the bonds that unite its members, are
the subject of vehement and incessant debate between
hope and fear. No disappointment, however cold, could
make the world after 1789 exactly what it was before, for
intimations strange and alien to the eighteenth-century
mind linger in the senses, although a blight had fallen
on the first promise of "the greatest and best thing that
had ever happened in the history of man." Between
Gibbon and Wordsworth fear and hope had both passed
through a revolution.

This was an atmosphere to excite thinkers and
dreamers, and we know how quickly the active minds,
philosophers and poets, turned to new problems in this
crisis of our history. The atmosphere that produced
Bentham and Godwin, Southey and Coleridge, Ricardo
and Malthus, Shelley and Wordsworth, Mill and Carlyle,
was certain to produce some intellectual movement in
the working-class world. We see the result in the appearance of thinkers and writers representing revolt in different aspects, Paine, Spence, Carlile, Hone, Hetherington, Cobbett who idealized the past the peasant was
losing, and Lovett who idealized the future that he saw
in the workman's grasp. It has been said that when the
licence enjoyed by Gibbon was claimed by Carlile a new
world had taken to infidelity; so when Cobbett's "Two-
penny trash" succeeded to the Letters of Junius a new
world had taken to politics. The characteristic of this
age was the cheap pamphlet or paper written for the
working man. At first this literature found its audience
chiefly among London shoemakers, small tradesmen,
and artisans, but in time it spread to the miners and the

mill workers; Lancashire was for Church and King in 1793, but for radical reform in 1819. It was said in the exaggeration of panic of *The Black Dwarf*, published by Wooler the Yorkshire printer who migrated to London, that in one northern district in 1819 it was to be found in the crown of the hat of almost every pitman you met. Ten years later the mills used to turn out when the London coach brought Cobbett's *Register* to the Lancashire towns. The first paper was published in London, but the provincial towns soon followed. Manchester had a *Wardle's Manchester Observer*; Birmingham, *Edwards' Weekly Register*; Coventry its *Recorder*; Dudley its *Patient*. In addition to the better-known papers, like Carlile's *Gauntlet*, Detroisier's *Cosmopolitan*, the Spencean paper *Man*, the Owenite paper *The Crisis*, the *Working Man's Friend*, there were several unstamped papers in the country, especially in Manchester, Leeds, Bradford, and such towns, taking their tone from the *Poor Man's Guardian*, owned by Hetherington and edited by Bronterre O'Brien. The *Pioneer* was the organ of the Builders' movement in the early thirties; Doherty ran *The Voice of the People* and the *Poor Man's Advocate*; and in 1837 Feargus O'Connor started the most successful of all the democratic papers, the *Northern Star*. Of the wild hopes about this new force that inspired democrats at the time, we have an illustration in the concluding verse of Ebenezer Elliott's poem, *The Press*:

> " 'The Press' all lands shall sing,
>   The Press, the Press we bring,
>   All lands to bless!
>   O pallid want! O labour stark,
>   Behold we bring the second ark,
>   The Press, the Press, the Press."

To understand what forces were ready to gather behind these rebel or these building minds, we must remember that the new towns were drawing into factory and slum men and women who had themselves passed through a revolution. Dr. Redford says that the census returns for 1851 show that in almost all the great towns the migrants from elsewhere outnumbered the people born in the town. Now the industrial towns were growing at a great pace. We can get an idea of the pace if we take the census figures for three years, 1801, 1831, and 1851, for some of the towns of Lancashire and the West Riding. The figures for Manchester and Salford are roughly 90,000, 237,000, 400,000; for Leeds, 53,000, 123,000, 172,000; for Sheffield, 46,000, 92,000, 135,000; for Bradford, 13,000, 44,000, 104,000; for Oldham, 22,000, 51,000, 72,000; for Bolton, 18,000, 42,000, 61,000; for Blackburn 12,000, 27,000, 65,000; for Halifax, 12,000, 22,000, 34,000. In all these towns and in many others a great proportion of the inhabitants had changed their home, their occupation, and their surroundings. Now the Industrial Revolution seen in the perspective of the life of the world may seem a gradual process, so gradual that economists find fault with the phrase as inexact. But as an experience in the individual and family lives of the men and women drawn into Manchester or Bradford, the Industrial Revolution was sudden and its consequences sweeping. The revolution that had given them a new home and a new manner of life would not have lost its sharp taste if the economist had explained to them that large-scale production was known in the ancient world, and that specialized industry had once enriched Babylon and Damascus just as it was then enriching Manchester and Bradford. The towns had now large populations of men and women who had passed from the life of the village to the life of the slum; from the occupations of the peasant to those of the urban worker.

The new population was mainly composed of people born and bred in the country. Wordsworth said that the invention of the steam engine had saved the country-side, for mills could now be built in the ugly towns instead of spoiling the streams and valleys. For the

country people turned into slum dwellers the change was
less fortunate. They had not lost their instincts and
longings or their sense for beauty and peace. Some observers think that we are paying the penalty to-day for
making our towns unsightly in the destruction of our
landscape by a town people in whom the sense for
beauty has been killed. It was feared in the thirties that
if London people found themselves in a park or garden
the "propensity to mischief" would assert itself with
disastrous results. In the North, on the other hand,
where the workman's memories of his country life were
still alive, observers noticed with astonishment that this
propensity was kept in check. When Lord Stamford
threw open his park on a Sunday the workpeople of
Manchester flocked there, making the journey in many
cases on foot, and the park suffered no damage at the
hands of 20,000 visitors. Sir Joseph Paxton told the
Committee on Public-Houses in 1854 that the Duke of
Devonshire allowed excursionists from Birmingham,
Nottingham, Leicester, and Leeds to visit Chatsworth,
and that their behaviour was most orderly. "As many
as 1,000 or 1,200 people go round at a time and in no
instance have we found any difficulty arise. . . ." "We
had only one man or perhaps two over the whole
premises to look after them; and the people behaved
exceedingly well." The love of nature dies hard. Léon
Faucher, a French visitor, who wrote a description of
England in 1845, said that one of the evils of which the
poor were most conscious in Leeds was the smoke that
destroyed their little window gardens.

Nor was the loss of beauty the only discomfort these
immigrants suffered. Wordsworth has described the lone
shepherd on a promontory.

> "Who lacking occupation looks far forth
> Into the boundless sea and rather makes
> Than finds what he beholds."

Nature gives some play to the fancy of the peasant as
his eye wanders slowly over field and woodland, and

though we picture him with a simple mind, town life, to make him happy, has to find some substitute for the satisfaction that the lone shepherd found in his promontory looking far forth into the boundless sea. For the first half of the nineteenth century the industrial town was absorbing the English peasant used to an open-air life, learning from the landscape, in touch with nature, moving and thinking with its gentle rhythm, making rather than finding what he beheld.

The towns were thus receiving a large population strange to town life in habits and experience. But there was an even more disturbing element in the problem now set to governments and magistrates, to architects and engineers, to doctors, schoolmasters, and ministers of religion. If you went to Manchester or Leeds, or to the smaller towns like Oldham or Stalybridge, you would find that the immigrants were in the main either countrymen from the same or a neighbouring county, or Irishmen and Irishwomen. It was easier to reach Lancashire and Yorkshire from Ireland than from Norfolk or Dorset. A Wiltshire peasant would have to make his way North by coach or canal boat or wagon, or on foot. The labourers who were sent to Lancashire by the Poor Law authorities were taken to London, put on a boat of Pickford's at the Paddington basin of the Grand Junction Canal, and carried to Manchester in four or five days at a cost of fourteen shillings. But an Irishman could cross to Liverpool for half a crown in fourteen hours; in 1827 fierce competition brought down the price to fourpence or fivepence.

Now Ireland so dangerously near to Lancashire was an uncomfortable neighbour. For the Irish peasant was the victim of unexampled misgovernment and neglect. "In no other country," said *The Times*, "have the wealth of the proprietor, the power of the magistrate and the accomplishments of the educated, been employed less for the benefit of the many, more for the gain and the pleasure of the few." Consequently the

Irish immigration had a special character. Sir George Cornewall Lewis pointed out that the Greeks and Phoenicians settling in the Mediterranean, the Spaniards and the English settling in the New World, went from a more to a less civilized community. The Fleming woollen weavers, the Huguenot silk weavers, the German tailors, brought to England, the English mechanics took to France, a special skill. "But the Irish emigration into Britain is an example of a less civilized population spreading themselves as a kind of substratum beneath a more civilized community."

This Irish substratum composed in 1841 a tenth of the population of Manchester and a seventh of the population of Liverpool. At that time the Irish population in Lancashire was over 133,000. But after the failure of the potato in the forties, the event that precipitated the repeal of the Corn Laws and the break-up of the Conservative party, the flood became a deluge. It has been calculated that 500,000 Irish people entered Great Britain between 1841 and 1851. By the later date the Irish population in Lancashire had nearly reached 200,000, swollen by the refugees flying from the famine that destroyed nearly a million lives in Ireland. "During the last two or three months," wrote the registrar of a Manchester district, "large numbers of the poor from Ireland have crowded themselves in this district, droves of them rambling about the streets seeking lodgings and no doubt being exposed to the severe and inclement weather. Many of the poor creatures have died from cold producing fevers and diseases." At Liverpool there were "thousands of hungry and naked Irish perishing in our streets," and in South Wales they were described as "bringing pestilence on their backs, famine in their stomachs."

Thus the dirtiness and disorder of the squalid English town were now increased by the presence of a large body of Irish people who lived normally under conditions repugnant to their English neighbours.

This had two serious consequences. In the first place, the greatest blot on the towns where the Irish settled was the cellar-dwelling. The immigrants crowded into these cellars and, as there was no check on the speculative builder, cellars were built in great numbers with the confident expectation of finding tenants for them. This was not the only evil that was prolonged and extended by the Irish immigration. The Irish immigrants in Lancashire, competing with a more skilled population, were confined as a rule to the coarser and less eligible employments. Among the occupations from which English workmen were turning away because its wages and prospects were steadily declining was that of handloom weaving. The Irish resorted to this failing industry and drew out its slow and painful death.

In these ways the Irish immigration was a burden on towns where filth and poverty were already unmanageable problems. But it brought also the friction that is inevitable when immigrant labourers can underbid the natives. As Irishmen were often bricklayers' labourers, and as they had been employed a good deal on roadmaking and canal-cutting, they were specially suitable for such work as railway construction. But by the late thirties, when railway projects were in great favour, trade depression had brought unemployment and there were riots in several places when attempts were made to introduce Irish labour. More than once such riots became battles, and it was often found impossible to put English and Irish to work together. That the Irish were used to keep down wages and to break strikes was admitted by textile employers, and Irish labour was brought over from Ireland for this purpose by a silk manufacturer at Newton Heath and by cotton spinners at Preston. The employers, however, regarded Irish workmen with mixed feelings, and they spoke of them sometimes much as a Roman master used to speak of the slaves from turbulent Sardinia. "The Irish," said one employer, "are more disposed to turn out, to make

unreasonable demands, to take offence at slight cause
and to enforce their demands by strikes or bad language." A Catholic priest said that he had noticed that
the Irish were more prone than the English to take part
in trade unions, and he attributed this to habits acquired
under the bad laws of Ireland. Whether this or the
Celtic temperament was the cause, it is undoubtedly
true that Ireland gave several leaders to the English
workmen, the most notable of them being, of course,
the celebrated John Doherty, the founder of the
strongest union of the time, whose services to reform
must be set against the social problems that his countrymen brought with them. The discord due to economic
friction was inflamed by religious differences. Nobody
can study the papers of this time without seeing how
widespread and violent were the religious quarrels of
the industrial towns.

The towns, then, to whom it fell to act as the civilizing influence in this new society were largely inhabited
by men and women who were country people by experience, taste, and habit, and in respect of great numbers,
alien in history, religion, and race. But it was not only
in this way that this population felt the strain of change.
There was at the same time a revolution in the life and
rhythm of industry. English industry before this time
was unmethodical. Bouts of work and bouts of play
used often to alternate, violent play following violent
work. Bamford has described the Christmas festivals of
his young days when beer was brewed and spice-cake
baked, and the weavers, young and old, kept at work
night and day to finish their tasks so that the days after
Christmas might be free for feasting and revelry. Even
in ordinary times whole days rather than hours in a day
were given to recreation. The Sheffield journeymen were
said to work only three days in the week. This is probably an exaggeration, but the custom of taking days off
even when work was plentiful survived in non-factory
industry. Thus the framework knitters at Hinckley sat

at their work for thirteen to sixteen hours a day, never
getting into the open air till twelve on Saturday, when
the work was sent to the warehouse and they stopped
completely till Tuesday. Monday was market day, and
the workers were fagged out. In the Potteries, too, the
custom survived, and in the country districts round
Coventry the ribbon weavers, however poor they were,
were said in 1840 to "absent themselves from work
nearly the whole of Saturday, Sunday, the whole of
Monday and a little of Tuesday," working excessively
hard for the rest of the week, including often the whole
of Friday night. These outbursts of work and play were
uneconomical, and, where machinery was introduced, a
new system of work was obviously necessary. Improved
methods of production involved the training of the
working population in orderly and regular habits. Fines
regulated every detail of conduct. To people accustomed
to the irregular and undisciplined atmosphere of the old
industry, the system of fines in the mills seemed gross
tyranny.

Here, then, were all the elements of a difficult social
problem. The towns were the homes of workmen, once
artisans with scope for their instinct to express and
create, who had passed into the impersonal routine of
the mill; of men and women with peasant outlook and
tradition, accustomed to the peace and beauty of nature,
shut up in slum and alley; of immigrants from a land of
deadly poverty, bringing their own habits and religion
into a society struggling with dirt and torn by sectarian
strife. All of these types were being drawn into new
associations, creating and receiving the influence of new
group atmospheres. We know to-day how subtle and
powerful is the influence of what Mazzini called "collective intuitions." The new town had thus to satisfy
the spiritual needs of men and women wrestling with
the most difficult of all spiritual adjustments, forming
a new social mind, disturbed by changes that had
destroyed the basis of custom in their lives. The evi-

dence of man's power in the world was impressive and
ubiquitous. The contrasts that religion had to justify,
the inequalities that culture had to reconcile, were glaring and provocative. How was this society placed for
that task? On what did it rely to draw these various
elements together in mutual sympathy and confidence?

CHAPTER IV

THE REMEDY OF THE NEW WORLD

INDIVIDUAL OPPORTUNITY

THIS society was not blind to the danger of discontent, nor was it unaware of the reasons for expecting that discontent to increase. De Quincey has an interesting passage in his description of his early life at Greenheys in Manchester about what he called personal Jacobinism. He and his brother, when on their way to school, used to meet a number of mill boys who called them "bucks" and pelted them with stones because they wore Hessian boots. De Quincey adds that however angry they were made by his aristocratic dress, the youths from the mill had no sympathy with political Jacobinism and would shout readily enough for Church and King. Their personal Jacobinism, he explained, was "of that sort which is native to the heart of man, who is by natural impulse (and not without a root of nobility, although also of base envy) impatient of inequality, and submits to it only through a sense of its necessity, or under a long experience of its benefits." De Quincey was speaking of the opening years of the century. Long before 1830 it had become evident that this personal Jacobinism was developing into political Jacobinism, and the problem of disarming or repressing this political Jacobinism had become the main care of the governments of the time. It did not follow because those governments neglected the methods used for this purpose by ancient societies that they had no methods of their own.

To understand what those methods were it is convenient to return to Bacon's distinction between rulers who seek to command the wills of men and those who seek only to command their deeds and services. The distinction is roughly between governments that seek to rule with the help of the imagination of the ruled, and those that seek to rule without it. That distinction divides both governments and politicians. In England in the early nineteenth century both schools were represented by men of vigour, courage, and tenacity. Both schools had been greatly strengthened by the French Revolution, which had confirmed in their convictions both the school that trusted entirely to force and the school that believed in governing men by persuasion.

The school of force refused to admit that society could be made happier or more stable by attempting to create a spiritual sympathy between government and governed, between class and class. A spokesman of this school, say Castlereagh or Sidmouth, would have said, if asked to explain his philosophy, something like this: "Life for the mass of men and women must inevitably be hard, bleak, and painful. Poverty is bearable by those who are used to it. Great economic and social changes are upsetting the life of custom, which is the life of acquiescence. For that very reason let us cling more closely to custom, where it can still be preserved, custom in government, custom in religion, custom in law. After all, the mass of men have obedience in their bones. The moment you begin to reform your capital institutions you destroy the attachment of custom, and you cannot make sure that you are going to create in its place ties of affection or confidence. Keep, therefore, what you have: an unreformed Parliament, unreformed law, unreformed Church, a landed aristocracy maintained by the Corn Laws. Use these institutions to make disobedience terrible to those who are tempted into it. But keep temptation out of their way. Do not let any disturbing or stimulating influence reach this subject population. Put down the cheap press; shut up agitators; leave the poor ignorant, or if you must teach them give them only such an education as will put the fear of

God and of the magistrates into their hearts. The more the inequalities of life increase, the more essential is it to see that government rests on an adequate force of power, tradition, and the prestige that belongs to superior culture. Look to this, and do not flatter your fancy with dreams of 'consenting peoples.' '' This school, strongly represented among politicians, churchmen, and magistrates, in the first twenty years of the century, had a powerful influence on the life of the times. It sought to crush the cheap press and popular propaganda by imposing heavy stamp duties on all periodicals, it put men in prison freely for distributing pamphlets and books, and Sidmouth would have liked to suppress all reading-rooms. At this time, as Dr. Hook said later, every sermon preached on behalf of a charity school had to prove that no harm would be done by educating the poor.

This school survived, of course, after 1830, but no longer as a political party; it was a die-hard faction. You would have found among landlords, manufacturers, magistrates, parsons, and other persons of influence, men who thought like Sidmouth and Castlereagh. But Peel, who led the Conservative party until he destroyed it, had nothing in common with this sentiment; he differed from a Tory like Sidmouth more than he differed from a Radical like Hume. The Conservative party in his hands was a party of reform, not of repression. Men disagreed in the value they put on existing institutions; on attachment to Church or squire; on the uses of custom or the dangers of change. But none of the greater leaders of thought or of politics would have held that their society could be ruled without the help of its imagination. Wordsworth or Coleridge, Maurice or Arnold, Carlyle or Mill, Peel or Russell, Bentham or Southey, all of them in their plans for improving or regulating the world rejected the garrison system of Sidmouth and Castlereagh, and aimed at commanding the wills and not merely the deeds of the ruled. The

motives of loyalty or ambition, of sympathy or rever-
ence, these, and not the spirit of fear, were the forces
to which the guiding minds looked for the salvation of
their society.

Among the ideas of the time one predominated in
the practical life of the time. It was the belief that the
Industrial Revolution had discovered the best remedy
for discontent. For it offered to the poor man something
to touch his imagination; something to stimulate the
element of nobility in the personal Jacobinism described
by De Quincey, and to discourage the base envy that
embittered it. It offered to him the prospect of ceasing
to be a poor man. For the Industrial Revolution had
put a new ladder within the reach of diligence and
worth. Never had men passed with steps so sure and
swift from poverty to wealth, from obscurity to renown.
To recite the names on this new roll of fame, from
Brindley to Stephenson, from Davy to Arkwright, from
Telford to Peel, is like reciting the names of Napoleon's
field-marshals, from Hoche to Murat, from Ney to
Bernadotte. Seen in this light, the cotton industry
offered to the English workman the prospect that the
revolutionary armies had offered to the French peasant.
When did thrift, enterprise, and intelligence reap such
reward?

It is true that men had found their way in other ages
from insignificance to power; that starting within the
Roman slave system a man might become a great
bureaucrat, a great doctor, a great man of letters; that
inscriptions tell us of a senator and censor who began
life as a clodhopper, of towns adorned and paved
by rich men who had once crept along their streets
behind a master with power of life and death; that in
the Middle Ages the Church offered an escape from the
drudgery of the soil to such men as the Minister Suger,
or Pope Silvester II; that in the sixteenth and seventeenth centuries banking and commerce could turn plain
homespun material into something that would pass for

the finished product of a proud and ancient line. But where in other ages there had been room for one man on this golden staircase, there was now room for a hundred. A merchant or a spinner like Gould or Cobden moved in a world where it was more likely than not that the first rich man he met had been born poor, and was, in Tiberius' phrase, his own ancestor. Peel, speaking against the Ten Hours Bill, said that he could name a dozen cases of men, once living on 20s. or 25s. a week, who now possessed fortunes of £100,000.

It was not only the railway king or the cotton lord who symbolized this triumphant principle for the optimists of the age. Cobden was enthusiastic about the ease with which a thrifty man could make himself independent without luck or genius. "I would then," he said in a famous letter, "advise the working classes to make themselves free of the labour market of the world, and this they can do by accumulating twenty pounds each, which will give them the command of the only market in which labour is at a higher rate than in England—I mean that of the United States. If every working man would save this sum, he might be as independent of his employer as the latter, with his great capital, is of his workmen." So simple a sacrifice was all that was needed to make the man who to-day looked the slave of his circumstances a person of standing, choosing his employment and his employer.

To understand how strongly this spectacle attracted the vigorous minds of the time, we must remember the history and tradition of the class that provided the leaders of thought and fashion in the new towns. The pioneers of commerce and industry, who had been gaining wealth and position with such steady progress in the last two centuries, had acquired from their experience definite habits of mind and character. The great commercial and industrial expansion of the seventeenth

and eighteenth centuries was due largely to the energy
of Nonconformists, who had been excluded or discouraged from a public career by the nature and sincerity of their religious opinions. The pioneers who laid
the foundations of the great metal industries were often
men who had suffered themselves, or whose fathers had
suffered, under Acts of Uniformity and other intolerant
laws. Unincorporated towns like Manchester and Birmingham offered a refuge to the uncompromising Dissenter
whose conscience would make no terms with Church
and State. The vigour and initiative on which the new
towns depended were largely to be found in men brought
up in this atmosphere, in men, that is, who had been
compelled by their circumstances to concentrate their
attention on one side of life.

Thus individual success took in this society the place
that common enjoyment had taken in the ancient world.
The business man, pointing to the triumphant career
of the Lancashire cotton spinner, with "nitor in
adversum" for his family motto, would have argued
that there was here a more inspiring spectacle, a truer
sign of human progress, than a theatre at Olympia,
crowded with Greeks of every class listening to a chorus
of the "Agamemnon." This ideal had the glamour and
freshness that belonged to a new religion, for it was
associated with the great emancipating truths that the
world had learnt from the French and American Revolutions. The freedom to make the most of yourself in
competition with your fellow men seemed to the Englishmen of the age the most important of all the personal
rights that those Revolutions had proclaimed and vin-
dicated. This right marked a great step forward in the
history of mankind. As individualism dethroned feudalism, the prestige of work dethroned the prestige of idleness. Now the prestige of idleness had been one of the
curses of the world. From time to time it had been
shaken. The monks, building their monasteries with
their own hands, had put to shame the false pride that

made a Roman think it less disgraceful to depend upon a State or upon a patron than to earn his living by the labour he called sordid. But the prestige of idleness had persisted through the world's history, and eighteenth-century England maintained gentlemen of good families, living on pensions and sinecures, who thought themselves morally superior to anyone who worked for his living. Herodotus explained why industrial occupations were despised in the ancient world in comparison with occupations or modes of life that fitted men and States for war. Manchester reflected the new light in which this false perspective had been destroyed: war and industry had changed places. What was the history of progress but the history of man's advance from a world in which wealth and power had been seized by those who had conquered and plundered their fellows, to a world in which they had been earned by those who supplied the wants of mankind? It had been a great day in that history when the merchants of Venice and the bankers of Florence were strong enough to make themselves the rivals of feudal lords and royal princes. With the new prestige of production a still more brilliant day had dawned. When men admired the Peels and the Arkwrights, they would soon estimate at their true value the Bourbons and Napoleons, the great drones or the great pirates, who had once cast such a fatal spell on the human mind.

The Manchester merchant would have argued also that the new industrial system had given the English people a flexible society. Movement from class to class is a sign of a healthy social life. Men were rising in the world in Cobden's Manchester by hard work, prudent abstinence, shrewd sense, and inspired daring. How had men risen in other ages? What were the arts by which slave and ex-slave had made their way to independence and power in the Roman State? Listen to Juvenal or to Tacitus on the climbing freedman. When a weak Emperor was on the throne, or a strong Emperor lost his power of will, the Roman Empire slipped into the hands of favourites and had all the look of a degenerate Oriental State. Seneca has described Claudius giving an order in heaven: "You might have imagined they were all his own freedmen; so little notice did they take of him." When the worst had been said about the forces and qualities that brought a man to the front in the early scramble of the Industrial Revolution, this method of promotion was at least to be preferred to the arts by which many a Roman Prefect had become a power in the government of the Roman Empire. The system which had made Peel the master of the House of Commons need not fear the comparison with the system which made a Pallas the master of the Senate.

Let anybody, again, compare this industrial England with feudal England: Manchester with the villages of Dorset and Wilts. Here men rose by their merit and by their own efforts. A man who had saved a few pounds could put his best foot foremost without touching his cap to any of the powerful men on whose pleasure Crabbe, or Porson, or Clare had had to wait. And the most active minds of the time had no liking for the historical institutions through whose doors poor men in other ages had passed to fame. Those institutions from the Church downwards were as remarkable at this time for their abuses as their virtues, and the spirit of the age welcomed as the solution of most of the problems of life an arrangement which seemed to make the individual his own master, and to reduce in proportion the prestige and the power of the institutions that offered at once discipline and shelter to those who would step across their threshold. The man who in other ages wished to follow in the footsteps of Wolsey had to put on the cassock of a church, but a Peel or an Arkwright could become a millionaire without the surrender of conscience or freedom to anybody's keeping. This was the novelty that fascinated men like Cobden. They contrasted this world in which men needed no patron with the world where everything depended on the smile of squire or parson, much as Lucian contrasted the free life of Athens with the degrading atmosphere of Rome, where flatterers courted the rich, and spoke to them as slaves spoke to a master.

Not least, perhaps, of the advantages that the Manchester merchant would have claimed for his age would have been its success in turning aside from the frivolities of the ancient world. For he would have regarded the social life of the Roman Empire as a warning rather than an example. Where had that social life ended? Dion Chrysostom scolded the people of Alexandria for their wild excitement over horse-racing. "For cities are not only taken when men demolish their walls, kill the men, enslave the women, and burn their houses. When there is indifference to all that is noble, and a passion for one ignoble end; when men devote themselves and their time to it, dancing, mad, hitting each other, using unspeakable language, often blaspheming, gambling their possessions, and sometimes returning in beggary from the spectacle, that is the disgraceful and ignominious sack of a town." Amid the orgies of the theatre at Carthage in the fourth century A.D., when Genseric's Vandals were outside the walls, "the voices of the dying were mingled with the voices of the revellers." Gibbon has drawn a graphic picture of the violence of the factions of the circus at Byzantium, and the fierce and bloody contests of green and blue that distracted the politics of the Eastern Empire. A sober merchant of Manchester would have laughed at the suggestion that his town, busy from rising to setting sun increasing the riches and comforts of the world, had anything to learn from a civilization that had degenerated into these scenes of outrage and discord, in which production had never been given its true importance, enjoyment had been allowed to run wild, and the men who served mankind the worst received the highest honours. Happy the new age in which success was so clearly the reward of merit, and private wealth and public benefit were so fortunately united. We have now to see what kind of town was created by these ideas; what was its education, its religion, its culture, and its social life.

CHAPTER V

THE STATE OF THE TOWNS

The quotations in this chapter are taken from the following sources:

> *Report of the Health of Towns Committee, 1840.*
> *Report of the Poor Law Commission on the Sanitary Condition of the Labouring Population, 1842.*
> *Reports of the Health of Towns Commission, 1844 and 1845.*

ABOUT the year 1840 those responsible for the government of England became painfully aware that during the preceding fifty years, in the course of an amazing growth of population, the proportions between town and country dwellers had completely changed; that, whereas in 1790 the country labourers were about double the town workmen, the town workmen were now nearly double the country labourers; that, in spite of the general advance in the arts and amenities of life, this new town population had what was graphically described as "a low and grovelling mode of living."

The cholera epidemic of 1832 called public attention to the subject of the towns, and late in the thirties and early in the forties there was a series of inquiries which throw a vivid light on the conditions of town life. An attempt will be made in the chapter to reconstruct from the sometimes redundant and sometimes scanty material some picture of what daily life was like for the inhabitants of these towns. First, we must remember in thinking of the new urban population that the recent developments in industry had gathered together masses

of men and women, not only to work in the industry for
which the particular town or district was noted, but also
to produce goods or supply services for those workers.
Tailors, shoemakers, butchers, bakers, druggists, green-
grocers, bricklayers, plasterers, masons, chimney-sweeps,
and many others, all flocked to the centres of population. Whatever the character of the population, shelter
of some sort had to be supplied. Where an existing town
like Leeds or Manchester formed the nucleus of the
settlement, there was further crowding in the already
overcrowded and insanitary quarters of the poor, but
growing suburbs soon encircled the old centre. In some
of the cotton and in many of the iron districts, villages or
towns were now planted for the first time in sparsely
populated regions. Under such circumstances the employers were often compelled to provide houses themselves.

Where the population swarmed into a town employers
could leave this task to the speculative builder. A
typical example of the result is given in a description of
the growth of the suburbs of Bradford: "an individual
who may have a couple of thousand pounds does not
exactly know what to do with it, having no occasion for
it in trade; he wishes to lay it out so as to pay him the
best percentage in money; he will purchase a plot of
ground, an acre or half an acre; then what he thinks
about is, to place as many houses on this acre of ground
as he possibly can, without reference to drainage or
anything, except that which will pay him a good
percentage for his money; that is the way in which
the principal part of the suburbs of Bradford has
sprung up."

The kind of building that paid the good percentage
was described as follows: "An immense number of
small houses occupied by the poorer classes in the
suburbs of Manchester are of the most superficial character; they are built by the members of building clubs,
and other individuals, and new cottages are erected with

a rapidity that astonishes persons who are unacquainted with their flimsy structure. They have certainly avoided the objectionable mode of forming underground dwellings, but have run into the opposite extreme, having neither cellar nor foundation. The walls are only half brick thick, or what the bricklayers call 'brick noggin,' and the whole of the materials are slight and unfit for the purpose. . . . They are built back to back; without ventilation or drainage; and, like a honeycomb, every particle of space is occupied. Double rows of these houses form courts, with, perhaps, a pump at one end and a privy at the other, common to the occupants of about twenty houses."

When we think of the new houses crowding together, we must bear in mind that there were no building restrictions or town-planning schemes to hamper the impulse for economy in material and space. Each man could do what was profitable in his own eyes, and could exercise his ingenuity in packing on each acre the greatest number of human beings at the smallest cost. Such building Acts as existed applied only to parts of London and to a few other towns, and were concerned with regulations about the thickness of party walls between houses, designed to prevent the spread of fires. In a few of the growing towns, where the land happened to belong to a single landowner of enlightened views, certain town-planning restrictions were enforced. But these places were an exception. Most notable among them was the cotton town of Ashton-under-Lyne, where the Earl of Stamford, who owned the town, made certain conditions about "good, firm, and substantial" building when he granted leases. Though the old parts of the town had narrow streets and crowded back-to-back houses, the new parts, some seven-eighths of the whole, were said to show great improvement. "Lord Stamford," we read in the 1844 Report, "takes especial care to have all new buildings erected in airy, well-formed streets, and in all cases where leases expire of premises in the old town, his Lordship invariably binds the new tenants to widen the streets when necessary to relieve the overcrowding."

At Huddersfield again, Sir John Ramsden, who owned the town, enforced wide streets and "good straight houses"; and in the Glossop district of Derbyshire, owned by the Duke of Norfolk, which was passing from rural to manufacturing conditions, "the land is laid out in regular form, under the personal superintendence of the agent or surveyor of the owner of the soil, with a provision for the requisite streets, avenues, passages, drains, sewers, and other conveniences."

A disastrous effect of abortive town planning was seen at Chorlton-on-Medlock, one of the growing suburban townships of the borough of Manchester, where the streets as originally planned were to be wide and airy, with a front street and a back street to each row of houses; but as the first row did not stretch from front to back, another row was wedged in back to back with it, so that the original street now became a front street to the second row. This use of space, originally designed for giving light and air, was carried to an extreme in the St. Giles district in London, where an originally large square was gradually filled up from circumference to centre with buildings, like the nests of boxes with which children play.

The Window Tax,* too, in spite of the fact that since 1825 houses with less than eight windows were exempted from its incidence, still served to discourage light and air. As every window over the eight which were not taxed cost on an average 8s. 3d. a year, even though the opening might be only a foot square, architects and builders of any houses bigger than small cottages were naturally encouraged to devise structures with as few openings as possible, and the result was recognized as disastrous even in a generation for which fresh air had many ter-

* First imposed as a temporary measure in 1696, finally repealed in 1851.

rors. In most new houses privies, closets, passages, cellars, and roofs were left without ventilation.

The worst consequences were seen in the northern towns such as Newcastle and Barnard Castle, where a large proportion of the poorer people lived in tenement houses which had known better days. In Barnard Castle four-fifths of the weavers and half of the rest of the working classes lived in large houses, one house sometimes containing fifty or more persons. The effect of the heavy charges on the tenement houses in Newcastle was described by a collector of assessed taxes who had been originally appointed in 1805. "No circumstance has contributed more to injure the habitations of the poor, and to diminish their healthiness, than the tax upon windows, the manner of its assessment, and the high duty upon window glass. . . . This heavy taxation naturally induced proprietors of such property to close up every window not absolutely necessary for light. Many of the staircases were so darkened that it became necessary to grope the way up them, at noon-day, as at night. The effect of this process upon ventilation was deplorable, and continues to operate to this day, for although the tax upon windows is considerably reduced, yet it falls heavily upon such houses."

Though the new districts and the new houses were squalid and unsightly, it is a nice question whether they were any worse than the older districts and older houses round which they grew. The new cottages round Manchester, as we have seen, were said to have neither cellars nor foundations. Round Leeds, on the other hand, the new cottages, though of flimsier structure than the old, were said to have larger rooms and cellars to keep them dry. Opinions differed as to whether it was better to live in a jerry-built house with larger rooms or in a house that was smaller but substantially built. In Bradford, pronounced by James Smith of Deanston, the well-known authority on sanitation, to be "the most filthy town I visited," it was stated that there was no

improvement in the "more recent arrangements for the
abodes of the working classes." But it is safe to say that
the worst overcrowding was to be found in the old quarters of existing towns. Manchester, Liverpool, London,
were hard to beat; Leeds could show districts where
overcrowding could hardly be carried further; but Nottingham was the worst example. Nottingham could not
grow easily, and it contained in a narrow space 11,000
inhabited houses laid out in narrow streets, many of
them "built in confined courts and alleys, the entrance
of which is usually through a tunnel from 30 to 36 inches
wide, about 8 feet high, and from 25 to 30 feet long."
Of the 11,000 houses, upwards of 7,000 were built "back
to back and side to side."

Overcrowding, however, was not the worst element
in what one observer called "the perhaps unavoidably
unpropitious position of the lower orders in densely
populated manufacturing districts." To describe the
greatest discomfort, it is necessary to deal, however
briefly, with the unpleasant but important subject of
refuse. The problem of living in a closely packed community is, as everyone knows, enormously complicated
by the question of how to dispose of refuse, especially
that most repulsive refuse which consists of the waste
products of the human body. Now, in considering how
this particular refuse was disposed of in the early nineteenth century, we must bear in mind that, as travellers
to China soon realize, it has a considerable value as
manure; if left in heaps to rot and ripen, it acts as a
strong fertiliser for the soil. In England, in the early
nineteenth century, farmers were glad to pay for it; it
was, in fact, "a property highly prized." In country
districts it was the regular custom to hoard it. Content-
ment, no doubt, sat spinning at her cottage door, with
a rich dung-heap beside her, which would either serve
to make her potato patch more productive or would
bring in a few shillings from a neighbouring farmer. So
long as there were not too many other cottages with

similar heaps close by, and provided that the heap did
not drain into the well, no one was much the worse;
but when similar heaps were scattered about in the
crowded quarters of Birmingham, or Leeds, or Liverpool, the consequences were dangerous as well as
disgusting.

Sometimes there was not even provision for a midden.
The cellar-dwellers of Manchester and Liverpool, some
eighteen thousand in each town, had nowhere to put any
refuse of any kind. It had to go either into the streets or
into the already overcrowded receptacles of neighbouring
courts. Dr. Duncan, the well-known Liverpool sanitary
reformer, writing in 1840, estimated, after a statistical
investigation, that not only the cellar-dweller, but a
very large majority of the working-class inhabitants of
that town, were in the same predicament. There were
whole streets of houses in Leeds where conditions were
no better. It was this state of things that provoked
Chadwick's famous outburst: "Such is the absence of
civic economy in some of our towns that their condition
in respect to cleanliness is almost as bad as that of an
encamped horde, or an undisciplined soldiery." After
describing the sanitary precautions embodied in certain
Army Standing Orders, he continued: "The towns
whose populations never change their encampment have
no such care, and whilst the houses, streets, courts,
lanes, and streams are polluted and rendered pestilential,
the civic officers have generally contented themselves
with the most barbarous expedients, or sit still amidst
the pollution, with the resignation of Turkish fatalists,
under the supposed destiny of the prevalent ignorance,
sloth, and filth."

Even where provision for sanitation was made it was
often grossly inadequate, and the arrangements for
clearing away the refuse were usually utterly defective.
It may be pleaded on behalf of the civic officers that
the ownership of this filth, as we have seen, was a vexed
question, and complicated the problem. Of the northern

towns, Newcastle, Sunderland, Shields, etc., an observer wrote: "No circumstances appeared to me more fruitful of nuisance and disease than the attempt to accumulate the refuse of such privies and dust-bins as there were, for the purpose of selling it to the neighbouring farmers. . . . The landlords and farmers were led to encourage undue accumulations, and the local authorities were too often prevented from exercising their power in such cases as came under their jurisdiction, from the feeling that they were depriving the poor of a valuable source of income. . . ." In the Midlands, again, the complaint was made that: "In none of the towns visited is there any system of contracts with scavengers or nightmen to clear away at proper stated periods all refuse, filth, and night-soil from the courts and small streets inhabited by the poorer classes." Each inhabitant made his own separate bargain, with disastrous results. Sometimes the midden was claimed as the landlord's perquisite. In the Lancashire towns the local Acts were said to have a clause "reserving the right of manure to the inhabitants of houses who are desirous to keep it."

As the towns grew the demand for this manure fell off. The cost of cartage to more distant fields swallowed up all profit, and it became necessary to pay to have middens or cesspools cleared out. The problem of what to do with London refuse became acute as the town spread and the regular dumping grounds were covered. When the new London University, Hyde Park Gardens, and Belgrave Square were built, useful places of deposit were lost. "They drive us out," complained a contractor in 1844, " . . . they say they do not like our men, and they do not like our carts; we are not very pleasant sort of people."

Meanwhile the spread of water sanitation was changing the nature of the problem. The use of water to flush away refuse led to an increase in the number of cesspools. Filth and corruption were at any rate out of sight, deep in the earth, and though the solid matter had to be cleared out at intervals, the liquid took care of itself by soaking away. London became a honeycomb of cess-pools. The architect in charge of the cutting of the Black-wall Railway described the results: "The soil in the immediate connexion with the houses and surrounding the foundations was so saturated from the cesspools as to be, in my opinion, in a worse condition than in dung-heaps." London spring water acquired a curious colour and taste, but, fortunately perhaps, coal-gas was often considered responsible for this. What was called, in 1834, "the increase of luxury and love of cleanliness which marks the present day," in other words, the increasing use of baths, made the problem more difficult, for cess-pools filled up too rapidly. A solution presented itself: Why not connect house drainage with the existing sewers and let everything be washed away together?

The term "sewer" is now so much bound up in our ears with house drainage that it is important to remember that the sixteenth-, seventeenth-, and eighteenth-century sewers were not constructed for anything of the kind. They were built to carry off the water from marshes and low-lying places—in other words, for surface land drain-age—and were under the management of some hundred different authorities, called "Commissions of Sewers." Henry VIII, in 1532, "like a virtuous and most gracious Prince, nothing earthly so highly weighing as the advancing of the common profit, wealth, and commodity of this realm," had first established them. The story of the inefficiency, and in many cases corruption, of the various London Commissions during the time that the town was spreading in the early nineteenth century has been told by Mr. and Mrs. Webb. It was into these sewers, constructed for surface water and managed by inefficient bodies, that house drainage, provided a sewer was near enough, was now discharged. The results of the new system were tersely described in 1840: ". . . the Thames is now made a great cesspool instead of each person having one of his own."

The change, of course, did not take place all at once, and the two systems long went on side by side. In Liverpool the Commissioners of Sewers forbade the connexion of house drainage with their pipes, though a good deal of filth got down from the streets, but in most towns people began to use the sewers for the disposal of house refuse. The results in manufacturing towns, where a river ran through the town and was used for water-power, were particularly disastrous. As the flow was stopped by dams or weirs, a series of huge open cess-pools was created. Leeds, Bradford, Halifax, Sheffield, Coventry, Derby, Birmingham, Manchester, all suffered alike. For those who lived near its banks the famous Bridgwater Canal was associated, not with the triumph of engineering skill, but with "disgusting odours" of which the victims complained to the trustees. Sanitary reformers urged that, since steam-power had largely superseded water-power elsewhere, the use of steam instead of water in establishments near rivers should be made compulsory, so that the water should be able to carry away its cargo unchecked. Even where no dams obstructed the flow, a slow stream produced much the same effect: "The sewers of Bolton empty themselves into the small rivers which wind sluggishly through the town, and yield to the air, in their passage, the most offensive emanations." The Serpentine itself, intended by the original designer of Kensington Gardens and Hyde Park as an ornamental water, became "an open sewer" which drained Kilburn, Paddington, and Bayswater. "It is, indeed," said John Martin the artist, "a scandal upon the greatest metropolis in the world, that the only place near it in which the public can bathe is an open drain to a populous district, the filthy bed of which, when disturbed by even a single bather, causes the most unwholesome and disgusting effluvia imaginable."

Apart from the contamination of rivers and streams, the new use of sewers for house drainage produced a

volume of sewer-gas. Most sewer pipes were not even
round: they were flat-bottomed, and laid with little fall,
so that great deposits were formed at intervals. When the
way was completely blocked these deposits were cleared
out, but before that happened they had generated quantities of sewer-gas which escaped either into the houses
connected with the sewers or through gratings into the
streets. The smell from these gratings was the cause of
much complaint. "I find it every day in walking," said
one witness, "as I dare say we all do, a very great inconvenience, to say the least of it." Proposals to provide shafts for ventilation in place of the street gulleys
were frowned upon by the sewer authorities who feared
that they would only lead to the bottling up of the gas,
and so increase the danger to their workpeople. "Ex-
plosions," said George Saunders, the Chairman of the
Westminster Commission, "are continually taking place
and our people are frequently sent to the hospital. Our
surveyor can show a specimen of an entire new skin to
his hand, and he had an entirely new skin to his face,
and laid up in a very dangerous state."

The escape of sewer-gas into the streets affected rich
and poor alike, but in other respects the poor were less
exposed to its dangers than the well-to-do whose houses
were connected with the sewers under the new system.
The "gentleman of distinction" who nearly abandoned
his house, "in consequence of the unpleasant smells
which were continually arising" but "arose in the
greatest strength whenever he had parties," was a case
in point. His drains were imperfectly trapped, and
"whenever he had a party there was a stronger fire in
the kitchen, and stronger fires in other parts of the house,
and the windows and external doors being shut, and a
greater draught created, larger quantities of the foul air
from the sewers rose up." This illustration was used
as a much-needed warning to the enthusiast who hoped
to solve the problem of refuse by connecting "the house
of the poor man" with the sewers. "When the door was

shut, and he sat down to enjoy his fireside, he would have a stench." As things were, the stench came from outside, and was perhaps less dangerous.

Street cleansing, like street paving, was originally considered to be an obligation on the householder. Both became gradually a municipal duty. In the case of street cleaning there are three stages: (1) the householder does (or neglects to do) the work himself; (2) the householder piles up the dirt and the scavenger removes it; (3) the scavenger both sweeps and removes the dirt, with the exception that the householder is still expected to sweep the footway in front of his house. In accepting accounts of the cleansing of particular towns considerable caution is needed. Dr. Southwood Smith described the experience of "a distinguished foreigner" who was sceptical of the statements in the Reports on Fever in the metropolis, because "from the cleanliness, neatness, and apparent healthfulness of the main streets and thoroughfares in London, he could not bring himself to believe that there could be large districts containing hundreds of thousands of the people allowed year after year to remain in such a neglected and poisonous condition." A visit to these places convinced him that the picture had been under-coloured. Dr. Lyon Playfair, who wrote a report on Lancashire towns for the 1844 Health of Towns Commission, inserted an illuminating table on the subject. Taking the ten towns, Liverpool, Manchester, Salford, Chorlton-on-Medlock, Rochdale, Preston, Ashton, Bolton, Bury, and Wigan, he set out in each case the authorities, the number of scavengers, the stated periods at which streets were cleaned, and various other facts. If we look only at the information about the stated periods at which the streets were cleaned, we find that Liverpool, Manchester, Salford, Rochdale, and Preston were cleaned once a week, Chorlton-on-Medlock thirty-eight times a year, whilst Ashton, Bolton, Bury, and Wigan had no regular intervals. Once a week sounds fairly satisfactory, but the question in a further column "Are Courts and Alleys cleaned?" is answered "No" for each of the ten towns.

These answers show that we must beware of thinking that the whole of a town was cleaned because a local Act gave powers of cleansing and scavenging to some authority or other. In the first place, the Act probably covered only certain streets, for the Lancashire towns were not peculiar in this respect. In Leeds, for example, in 1842, out of a total of 586 streets, 68 streets were said to be "the only ones which are under any regulation, whether as to paving, draining, sewering, or cleansing." In Bradford, again, with its population of nearly 100,000 in 1840, street cleansing was "attended to" only in the actual township, for the local Act did not touch the suburbs, "by far the largest portion of the town." In Shrewsbury and Norwich only the old parts, within the walls, were cleansed; all over England, in town after town, courts and alleys were looked on as "private property."

In the second place, local Acts were not always carried out. Manchester illustrates this point. To say that under the local Act of 1791, which appointed Police Commissioners for Manchester, the streets were swept twice a week, sounds well on paper, but a study of the local records shows it to be misleading.

Dr. Playfair proved, by comparing the number of scavengers and the number of streets in Manchester and Liverpool, that the public streets could only be cleaned in Manchester once a fortnight, in Liverpool once every three weeks. The actual regulations in force till Whitworth's sweeping-machine was introduced in 1844 were that first-class streets should be swept once a week, second-class streets once a fortnight, third-class streets once a month, courts, alleys, etc., not at all. It is not surprising that when a statistical investigation was made in the township of Manchester by District Boards of Health, during the cholera alarm of 1832, it was found that in 352 out of 687 streets visited there were "heaps of refuse, stagnant pools, ordure, etc."

What happened, it may well be asked, in the courts and alleys which the scavengers did not visit? Apart from that cleansing "which Providence showers from the clouds," their state seems to have depended on the initiative and resource of the inhabitants. In Liverpool they sometimes remained a whole year uncleaned. At the end of that time the pile of muck and ashes might be worth a contractor's while to remove. In Birmingham people often tipped out their refuse from the courts by nights into the streets. Newcastle was not the only town where it was possible to talk of "that mass of filth that constitutes the street."

Such were the surroundings in which the new town population lived. What was life like for the housewife? An old judgment declared that "three great commodities" were essential to a man's house: "air for his health, light for his profit, prospect for his pleasure." Prospect and light were scarce enough in the crowded quarters, and air was none too common in the houses of the poor with that "close unpleasant smell" of which their betters complained. In many cases the excuse, "were the closed windows opened, it would frequently be only to admit a worse compound, the air from neglected privies, and the miasma from the wet and undrained court or street," might be valid, but it must be admitted that however pure the air outside, there was then, even more than now, a strong prejudice among rich and poor alike against admitting it to their houses. Fresh air was well enough in its place—out of doors. The description of the agricultural labourer at home applied to all classes: "He appears to be insensible to anything but changes of temperature, and there is scarcely any stench which is not endured to avoid slight cold." It was sometimes assumed that the objection to fresh air was increased by the habit of working in heated factories, but it is hard to believe that any factory was worse than the tailor's shop of which the master cheerfully said, "Oh, there is no necessity to take particular means to warm it, the

animal heat brings it up high enough," or the stocking-
weaver's shed where a weaver explained that it was impossible to open the windows during the fourteen or
sixteen hours' work, for it "would not be prudent as
our confinement makes us susceptible of cold."

It must be remembered that the open window was
counted a danger by current medical opinion, and the
Scottish doctor who used to "begin his prescription by
breaking a pane or two of the window with his walking-
stick, which he made good again at the end of the ill-
ness," was before his time. Children might faint from
the foul air in school, but the teachers were commended
for keeping the steaming windows tightly closed. Fresh
air, indeed, was advised, but in very moderate quantities. "Windows," wrote one medical authority, " . . .
are not recommended as affording the best means of in-
suring ordinary ventilation, though they may be resorted to with advantage when the weather is not severe,
or under peculiar circumstances, and should therefore
always be available when large supplies of air are required." What is needed, he explains, is "a much less
extended opening." The Sanitary Reports of the time
are full of ingenious devices for "mechanical ventilation," which will introduce a sufficiently small amount
of air.

Air, then, the poor neither had nor wished to have;
but there was another "commodity," water, which they
certainly desired, but did not obtain. The dearth of it
made life a hard struggle for the housewives who tried
to keep up some standard of cleanliness. It was generally
assumed that country people were cleaner than towns-
folk, but in the country a little washing went a long
way, and it was possible to produce a cleanly appearance with a very small amount of water. In the towns,
on the other hand, there was dirt in the streets and,
worse still, dirt in the air; torrents of black smoke took
all heart out of the housewife. Water was seldom close
at hand, and the labour of fetching it in quantities suffi-

cient to keep person and house clean became a weary task. "The whole family of the labouring man in the manufacturing towns," wrote Chadwick, "rise early, before daylight in winter-time, to go to their work; they toil hard, and they return to their homes late at night. It is a serious inconvenience, as well as discomfort, to them to have to fetch water at a distance out of doors from the pump or the river on every occasion that it may be wanted, whether it may be in cold, in rain, or in snow. The minor comforts of cleanliness are, of course, forgone, to avoid the immediate and greater discomforts of having to fetch the water." It is no wonder that the suggestion was made that "it is only when the infant enters upon breathing existence, and when the man has ceased to breathe—at the moment of birth and at the hour of death—that he is really well washed."

Often it was necessary to pay water-carriers, or to buy water from carts. Mr. Thomas Ashton of Hyde, the benevolent cotton employer, put water into the colony of 320 houses, where his workpeople lived, and found that whereas they paid $3d.$ a week for his good supply, they had formerly paid at least $1d.$ a day, and some as much as $1s.$ a week, to water-carriers for a small quantity. In Leeds some families paid as much as $2s.$ a week for water from carts. The charge per gallon varied considerably in different places; at Chorlton-on-Medlock and at Bradford, $1d.$ was charged by the carts for three gallons; in Preston, where there was competition with the waterworks, the charge was $\frac{1}{2}d.$ for three gallons; in Nottingham, before the regular supply was introduced, the charge varied from $\frac{1}{4}d.$ to $\frac{1}{2}d.$ a bucket according to distance; in Carlisle, water was sold at $1d.$ for eight gallons. In the squalid pages of the inquiries of the time, the tale of the spring at Frome which supplied a hundred families stands out. It was the property of "a man in humble life, named Flower, who, though possessed of little else than it, freely gives its waters to all who ask, denying no one. He even supplies his poor neighbours with cups and bowls, with which to dip the water out of the spring."

In towns where there was an organized water-supply in pipes, the water might be better and purer, but it was seldom laid on to working-class houses, and the business of fetching it was more difficult than in the case of wells or rivers. The supply was usually intermittent, and it was distributed to poor quarters by means of stand-pipes, one to some fifteen or more houses, out of which water poured for half an hour or an hour twice or thrice or oftener in the week. In Liverpool, for example, where the water was "pure and good," we read that "in the poorer neighbourhoods there is usually a cock in each court, and the inhabitants carry it and store it in jugs or wooden vessels from day to day; but, compared with the dense population, the supply is totally inadequate, as the turn-cocks of the company cannot allow it to run a sufficient length of time; and many of the habitations of the poor (whether from this circumstance or from inherent habits of filth, I do not venture to say) have never had their boarded floors properly scoured since the houses were erected. Many of the poor beg water— many steal it. . . ." "How do people get their water, when they are out at work?" a London witness asked. "They generally have some of their children at home," he answered, "to empty it into a tub, or something of that kind. To the better sort of tenants we give a water-tub; but in cases where they have no water-tubs or water-tanks, some of the family must be at home to take it in." The fetching of water did not lead to good relations among neighbours: "I have seen as many as from 20 to 50 persons with pails waiting round one or two stand-pipes. Then there is quarrelling for the turn; the strongest pushing forward, and the pails, after they are filled, being upset." There were lively scenes in Snows Rents in Westminster, where the one stand-pipe that supplied sixteen houses was turned on for about five minutes on Sunday, the principal cleaning day.

There were four grades of water storers: the lowest had only a tea-kettle or a saucepan or jugs to store it in; the next grade bought a butter-tub, costing 1s. and holding 8 gallons; the third grade rose to the purchase of a pork-tub for 2s. 6d., this held 42 gallons; the highest grade, "those who wish to be quite comfortable," invested from 16s. to 20s. in a wine-pipe, which held some 125 gallons. The wine-pipes were used in a few houses of a better description, where water was laid on in the yards. Sometimes the landlord provided the water-butt.

Two towns enjoyed an honourable distinction in respect of their water-supply. In Preston and Nottingham the houses might be overcrowded and insanitary and the death-rate might be high, but life, while it lasted, must have been made much more tolerable than in most places by abundance of water. In both towns the water was always on, and in Nottingham two-thirds of the houses were supplied. The manager of the Preston Water Works strongly advocated a constant supply with taps as more economical than the intermittent supply of running water customary elsewhere.

How much water was needed in a town to keep a house and family reasonably clean? A civil engineer, who had considered the matter carefully, declared that in London the actual consumption of "the family of an English workman of the cleanest kind," consisting of five persons, was under 20 gallons a day, or four gallons a head. Of the 20 gallons, 10 were used for cooking and personal washing. The other 10 were used for washing the rooms, washing the linen, and watering the flowers. The experience of Nottingham and Preston, however, showed that when water came to the door it was consumed in double that quantity. In Nottingham the average consumption of the labourer's family was estimated at 40 gallons a day; in Preston at 45 gallons a day.

It it interesting to speculate how far cleanliness is a natural and agreeable state for which sacrifices are

willingly made, or how far dirt is natural and cleanliness
an acquired virtue. The Rev. Whitwell Elwin, Chaplain to the Bath Union, a man doubtless of considerable
experience, was a strong champion of the latter view.
After explaining that even in "gentlemen's houses"
shifts were resorted to in order to avoid the cost of an
extra pail of water, he continued: "With the poor, far
less obstacles are an absolute barrier, because no priva-
tion is felt by them so little as that of cleanliness. The
propensity to dirt is so strong, the steps so few and
easy, that nothing but the utmost facilities for water can
act as a counterpoise; and such is the love of uncleanli-
ness, when once contracted, that no habit, not even
drunkenness, is so difficult to eradicate." But on the
other side there rise up to confute him those clothes-lines
of Leeds, where, on the weekly washing-day, half the
streets in the township were "so full of lines and linen
as to be impassable for horses and carriages, and almost
for foot passengers"; a danger to traffic, no doubt, but
the symbol of a gallant struggle against almost over-
whelming odds.

It was difficult, as we have seen, to wash at home, and
there were few towns where it was possible to wash elsewhere. The price of such baths as existed was usually
prohibitive. Liverpool was an exception, after 1842, for
in that year the Corporation started baths and wash-
houses where 2d. was charged for a warm bath, 1d. for
a cold bath, and 1d. for the use of a tub and hot water
for washing clothes. The chief credit for this reform is
due to an Irish immigrant, Mrs. Kitty Wilkinson, a poor
woman of noble character who offered the use of her
kitchen to her neighbours in the cholera epidemic for
washing their clothes. William Rathbone, who knew of
her successful enterprise, persuaded the Corporation to
establish public baths and put her in charge of them.
Her remarkable career has been commemorated in a
window in Liverpool Cathedral. At Leeds in 1842 there
was said to be a large swimming-bath owned by a private

company, open to the working classes every Saturday for 2d., and in Westminster an enterprising proprietor conducted with success an establishment with two swimming-baths side by side: one at 1s. for the middling class, the other at 3d. for mechanics. The water for the middling-class bath was being continually replenished, and then passed through a filtering bed into the bath for the "humbler classes." But these baths were exceptions, and as a rule the only bathing possible was in the rivers and canals, too often polluted by sewage or industrial refuse.

The medical men whose evidence forms so large a part of the 1844 Health of Towns Report took a more kindly view of shortcomings in cleanliness than some of the observers who lived under the shadow of the Poor Law Commission. They realized that the work of fetching and storing even 20 gallons of water is considerable, and that to empty out dirty water when there are no proper sinks takes time and energy; they could sympathize with the plea: "We are so knocked up with the day's work that the water must wait until to-morrow when we shall be able to remove it." Even in Bristol, where "the dwellings of the lower classes" were said by Dr. Lyon Playfair to be "generally abominably filthy, full of vermin, and in a condition such as I have not seen in any of the large towns of Lancashire," he ascribed it "wholly to the want of means, and not to any inherent habits in the people themselves, from whom we, in very many instances, received loud complaints on this subject." Bristol was particularly badly off for water; except in the case of the wealthy inhabitants, its large population depended on scanty supplies from public or private wells; of one private well it was reported that the owner "is obliged to pump twice a week with a steam-engine for the poor, in self-defence, for they rush in and take the water by pails."

The housewife had other difficulties besides want of water. In summer, we read of the Derby courts and

yards, "the passages are covered with creeping insects,"
and the swarms of flies, bred in the universal refuse
heaps, can be easily imagined. The discovery that flies
cause disease was not made till modern times, and nobody then connected them with the unquestionable fact
that town-dwellers were forced to live from hand to
mouth because no food would keep. The much-praised,
prudent housewife, with her little store of provisions,
was only to be found amongst the ill-paid agricultural
labourers; if she moved into a town, though earnings
might be doubled, prudence was useless; meat turned at
once, butter became rancid, bread became "dry and
disagreeable."

Man's life in crowded towns was bad, but woman's
was infinitely worse; it was the housewife who suffered
most from the misery of defective sanitary arrangements, and from the constant struggle with dirt. That
so many kept up some standards of decency and comfort is a marvel. Of the efforts made in the Yorkshire
manufacturing towns, James Smith of Deanston gave
a moving picture. "In the perambulation of the lower
districts inhabited by the poorer classes, it was often
very affecting to see how resolutely they strove for
decency and cleanliness amidst the adverse circumstances; to see the floors of their houses and the steps
washed clean, made white with the hearth-stone, when
the first persons coming into the house must spoil their
labours with the mud from the street, kept filthy by neglect of proper scavenging; to see their clothes washed
and hung out to dry, but befouled by soot from
the neighbouring furnaces; and to see their children,
attempted to be kept clean, but made dirty from
the like causes; and sometimes to see those children, notwithstanding all their care, pale, sickly, and
drooping, evidently from the pestilential miasma of a
natural stream converted into a sewer, and dammed up
for the sake of mill-power, in the hands of persons of
great influence in the return of members to the town

council, who are deaf to all statements of evidence of the evil, or of the possibility of amendment.''

Many failed, and their case is put with sympathy and insight by R. A. Slaney: ''Amidst these scenes of wretchedness, the lot of the female sex is much the hardest. The man, if, as is usually the case, in employment, is taken away from the annoyances around his dwelling during the day, and is generally disposed to sleep soundly after his labours during the night; but the woman is obliged to remain constantly in the close court or neglected alley where she lives, surrounded by all the evils adverted to; dirty children, domestic brawls, and drunken disputes meet her on every side and every hour. Under such circumstances, the appropriate employments of a tidy housewife in brushing, washing, or cleansing seem vain and useless efforts and she soon abandons them.'' Whether they struggled, or whether they abandoned the struggle, soured tempers and peevish complaints were the result of continual frustration. The melancholy of the town populations and their lack of animal spirits were conspicuous. It is almost a relief to read the description of the ill-cared-for house at Ashton-under-Lyne, where the mother went out to work; squalid children might sprawl ''on the flags, near the fire in danger of being burnt,'' the chairs, tables, stools and culinary vessels might be ''in dirt and disorder,'' but at any rate there was the gay sight of ''two or three young nurses and their friends playing at shuttlecock and other games.''

A cynic might say that it was the Irish, with their low standards of cleanliness and comfort, who best adapted themselves to the conditions of town life. They found dirt, and they multiplied it lavishly, but they preserved a contented spirit however degraded their surroundings, and their very recklessness helped them to keep clear of the trade in opiates, or the dealings with burial clubs, which formed a constant temptation to overwrought and harassed mothers.

One fact must always be borne in mind in any attempt
to picture the lives of the new industrial populations:
they were in the main country folk by feelings and
tradition, with their roots in fields and not in streets or
courts. "A great deal of their pallid and care-worn
appearance," said an acute observer of the inhabitants
of Manchester, "is not so much to be attributed to the
factory system, as it is to be attributed to the sweeping
together of large masses of people, with little intelligence,
under circumstances so unfavourable." These people,
he explained, "were not brought up in or prepared for
the new circumstances in which they have been placed."
One illustration will serve to show what this change
meant: In the Appendix to the First Report of the
Health of Towns Commission there are some plans and a
vivid picture of a new suburb that was growing up on
the outskirts of Preston. With an eye to the future the
builder has economized space, and set down in the fields
two rows of eleven houses, each with a minute back-
yard. The yards of the one row back on to the yards of
the other row, separated only by a long and narrow fosse
or ditch, four feet deep, which acts as an open cesspool
for these twenty-two houses and for four more houses
which are built up at one end of the two rows. "The
surface of refuse and decomposing matter," says the
Report, "exceeds 3,000 square feet." Any visitor to
this settlement would be aware of what Slaney once
called "the absence of the decencies of life and the constant presence of disgusting and dirty objects." And
yet the inhabitants of these squalid houses had something of which the town populations were deprived. "One
woman expressed her great satisfaction at having removed from Albert Street to her present abode: it was
'so pleasant to hear the birds singing in a morning, and
to see the flowers growing in the spring.'"

CHAPTER VI

THE LOSS OF PLAYGROUNDS

In England it is not only children for whom play seems to be a necessity of life. A modern wit has drawn the English character abroad in an epigram: "One Englishman a fool; two Englishmen a football match; three Englishmen the British Empire." This taste for games is not a recent development. Chamberlayne, writing on the English people in 1660, remarked that "the common people will endure long and hard labour, insomuch that after twelve hours' hard work, they will go in the evening to football, stockball, cricket, prison base, wrestling, cudgel playing, or some such like vehement exercise for their recreation." At all times there have been critics who have accused the English people of thinking their play more important than their work.

As industry turned country into town in the early nineteenth century, this national habit was checked and repressed in a drastic manner, for old playgrounds disappeared and new playgrounds were not provided. This change did not pass unnoticed, for an active and public-spirited member, R. A. Slaney, brought the subject before Parliament, and secured the appointment in 1833 of a Select Committee to consider the deficiency of "Public walks and Places of Exercise." The facts were presented to Parliament by this Committee. "As respects those employed in the three great Manufactures of the Kingdom, Cotton, Woollen, and Hardware, creating annually an immense Property, no provision has been made to afford them the means of healthy exercise or cheerful amusement with their families on their Holidays or days of rest." Nor did the Committee find other large towns in any better case. Of all but a very few they wrote: "With a rapidly increasing Population, lodged for the most part in narrow courts, and confined streets, the means of occasional exercise and recreation in the fresh air are every day lessened, as inclosures take place and buildings spread themselves on every side.'' This neglect, suggested the Committee, might be due to preoccupation with the late war. A century later it is easy to see that this is too simple an explanation, and that there were strong forces at work which public opinion, even when unpreoccupied, was powerless to control.

In a community where there is plenty of waste land and games are rude and uncomplicated, those who wish to play can easily find a playground. The people who live near what is called a common have no doubt that they can use it for recreation, whether stock is turned out on it or not by the Lord of the Manor and commoners. No questions of legal ownership trouble their minds. The difficulties begin when land rises in value, for legal rights then become important and the inhabitants become aware, from painful experience, of what has been called ''the difference between popular conceptions and traditions and legal rights and conclusions.''

According to the legal view which ignored ancient tradition and relied upon the imposition of the feudal system as the starting-point of common rights, all rights of common came from the grant or permission of the Lord of the Manor who owned the soil of the common or waste. It might have been argued that since the lord owned the soil in virtue of a grant which carried with it the performance of certain duties, the whole position should have been revised when those duties lapsed. But it was not revised, and in the eyes of the law the framework of feudalism still stood intact. Common rights, the right of use and the right of access, came into being, said the law, because at some time or other the lord had granted his tenants the right to graze cattle or sheep or to cut wood or turf on the waste of the lord's manor. It was then from the lord's grant or permission or sufferance that all common rights were derived.

Now in a famous case in 1603 (Gatewards case) it was laid down that these rights could not be held by the inhabitants of a village or district merely as inhabitants. The term, said the judges, was too vague; common rights could only be held by owners of property. "According to the strict technical law," said Lord Eversley, "invented by the feudal lawyers—and superseding a much wider and more popular law, under which undoubtedly the commons were the common property of the village or community—the commons were the property of the Lords of Manors, and the tenants of their manors, and the public had no right to them, no matter how long or how much they had used them for recreation, no matter how necessary they might be for the health of the district." The legal position was clearly put by a member of the 1844 Committee of Inclosure: "Notwithstanding that all the world are in the habit of walking about on commons, and turning themselves on, in fact they have not acquired any legal right by that, but, practically, they would lose something if they were deprived of it."

It would seem reasonable to expect that old paths and rights of way across land that came under enclosure would remain intact even if the public were no longer free to use the common. But this was not the case. In Enclosure Acts the Commissioners were usually empowered, or rather ordered, to take the map of the area to be enclosed, wipe out existing ways (turnpike roads sometimes excepted), and refashion the whole highway system. When they had done their work, any paths that did not appear in the map attached to their award ceased automatically to be rights of way.

An illustration will show that this legal interpretation of the rights of property put into the hands of the landowners in many places an almost unlimited power of depriving a community of its customary places for walks and games. We will take the case of Basford, a small framework-knitting town a few miles north of Nottingham, with 1,200 acres of forests, commons, and waste lands at its doors. Before 1793 the inhabitants probably never thought about their playgrounds or wondered how they had been provided; they took them as a matter of course. After 1793 there were no playgrounds to think about, for an Inclosure Act swept the whole area into private hands. The inhabitants of Basford did not easily adapt themselves to the changed conditions. Fifty years later it was stated (before the Health of Towns Commission) that the want of open land for recreation was "a fruitful source of bickering and recrimination between the young men of the parish and the owners and occupiers of lands, trespasses on the part of the young men, for the purposes of cricket-playing and other games, being very common. There are now no common lands belonging to the parish. Formerly there were very extensive grounds of this class, but in 1793 these rights were resumed and the grounds enclosed, but without leaving a single acre for the use of the public."

At Basford the disaster was catastrophic; in other cases, Sheffield for example, the process was spread over several years. In that town, by four separate Acts of Parliament, the first passed in 1799, the last in 1810, not less than 7,350 acres of common and waste lands were enclosed without a single rod, pole, or perch being set apart for public recreation. Enclosure of one common was made easier by the fact that a second remained open; enclosure of the second made easier by the precedent of the first. Enclosure Acts, it may be noted, were usually justified on the ground that the land was in its present state "incapable of improvement," whereas, if enclosed and handed over to private ownership, it would yield bounteous harvests. Round towns the big proprietors, and sometimes the small ones, too, easily persuaded themselves that crops of villas (or slums, as the case might be) were as desirable to grow as crops of corn.

Incidentally, they were considerably more profitable to the grower.

How little the need for recreation had been recognized in the growing districts is illustrated in the case of enclosures at Bolton, Oldham, and Gateshead. A great deal of waste was enclosed in East Lancashire before this time, in the sixteenth and seventeenth centuries, by agreement or moral compulsion. Didsbury Moor, Withington Moor, Kersal Moor, and Chorlton Moor, and other waste land near Manchester, had been enclosed by the eighteenth century. But there were Acts for enclosing wastes at Bolton and Oldham at the time when these towns were growing very rapidly. The Bolton Act, dated 1792, contains rare, if not unique, provisions for applying the proceeds of enclosure to public purposes. Unfortunately, recreation was not amongst those purposes. Although Great and Little Bolton were described in the Act as "large, populous, and trading Towns, and daily increasing," they were still large villages surrounded by open country. The Act directed that the 270 acres of Bolton Moor should be enclosed and, after allotment of one acre for stone and one-fifteenth for the Lords of the Manor, should be divided up into lots of not more than four acres and sold for 5,000 years for the best annual rent offered, subject to the immediate payment of £10 an acre. The money was to be spent by trustees, who were given large powers by the Act, on widening, paving, lighting, watching, cleansing, and otherwise improving the streets of Great Bolton, and on supplying water for the free use of the inhabitants. Any surplus was to go to the Poor Rates. Seventy-one trustees were appointed to administer the Act, forty-one for Great Bolton, with a residential qualification of £1,000, and thirty for Little Bolton, with a qualification of £5,000. Two other Enclosure Acts of the usual type swallowed up other moorland in the Bolton district: Chew Moor (68 acres) was enclosed in 1807, Tonge Moor (acreage not stated) in 1812. In neither case was any allotment made for recreation. The result was described in 1833. "The population of Bolton being nearly 45,000, there are no public walks, or open spaces in the nature of walks, or public gardens reserved at all in its vicinity?" "No." But though no part of the moor was reserved for the purpose, games were still allowed on sufferance on ground that was technically enclosed.

The case of Oldham is specially interesting. An area of 300 Lancashire acres (that is, about 480 ordinary acres), consisting of Green Acres Moor, North Moor, Hollingwood, and other commons and wastes, was enclosed in 1802 without any allotment for recreation. Public interests, however, were not ignored, for 16 acres were allotted for a workhouse. It happened that Oldham was already well provided in this respect, and the land so reserved was left idle. In 1826 another Act was passed. The population of Oldham had nearly doubled in the interval, and the case therefore for reserving this land for recreation was very much more pressing. The promoters of the Bill recognized the fact of this increase, but they asked for, and obtained, an Act, not to make provision for recreation, but to enable the churchwardens and overseers to let this site for building land in aid of the rates, since Oldham "hath become very populous and is rapidly increasing in population."

At Gateshead 600 acres of Gateshead Fell were divided by an Act passed in 1809, without any allotment being made for any public purpose, except one acre for a church and churchyard. On the enclosure of a further 200 acres of commonable land in 1814, the Windmill Hills, an area of about 10 acres, were left open and vested in the borough holders and freemen. It was disputed later whether this land belonged to its holders as their private property, on which they could build houses, or was, as the Corporation argued, merely vested in them for the benefit of the public. Gateshead, meanwhile, was reported as being in great need of public walks. The question was not finally settled till 1861,

when the borough holders handed over the ground to
the Corporation, under a deed, with stipulations that it
should be made an agreeable place of resort to the
public.

Blackburn affords a case where the need for recreation was recognized in the early seventeenth century, but
forgotten later. In 1618 the 1,266 acres of common and
waste lands were enclosed and divided up amongst the
owners of land in Blackburn, but some 18 acres were to
be set out and used "for the mustering and training of
people in that part, and for the recreation of the Inhabitants of the said Town, and for the good and profit of
the said Town and Poor thereof, as a gift for ever. . . ."
But the rights of recreation seem to have been lost by
1833, for when William Feilden, M.P. for Blackburn,
was asked by the Committee on Public Walks: "Is
there any place to which the children of the humbler
classes may resort for any game or exercise, any of those
games they have been used to on holidays?" his answer
was: "None whatever."

The records of parliamentary enclosure are unsatis-
factory, but of unparliamentary enclosure there are no
records. If a Lord of the Manor could gain the
acquiescence or the silence of the commoners, either by
buying up their common rights or in some other
fashion, there was no legal obstacle to the enclosure of a common. Nor was there any obstacle
till 1926. The process can be watched in later times,
when a vigilant searchlight was turned on it by the
public-spirited founders of the Commons Preservation
Society. There is no reason to think that in earlier days
Lords of the Manor were less acquisitive, or the costs of
opposing them less prohibitive.

Apart from deliberate enclosures, as towns grew,
opportunities for recreation were restricted by the
advance of building on land in private hands. Thus, in
Birmingham, though there were no parks, no public open
spaces, or common lands, yet in the early nineteenth

century a considerable portion of the population had
gardens of their own. ". . . It is the custom of Birmingham," said a witness in 1833, "for the working men to
have gardens at about a guinea a year rent, of which
there are a great number round the town, and all the
better parts of the workmen spend their leisure hours
there; a considerable portion of land in the immediate
vicinity of Birmingham is let at £12 an acre for these
small gardens." "Are they enabled," he was asked, "to
go there with their children?" "Their children and families," was the answer; "they have little summer-houses,
where they spend their evenings and Sundays." Nine
years later it was reported that the gardens in which
the mechanics "took great delight" were "now for the
most part built over, and the mechanics of the town are
gradually losing this source of useful and healthy recreation." The Spitalfields weavers suffered the same loss.

Nowhere was the neglect of any provision for exercise
and open-air amusements more striking than in Manchester. The commons and wastes of the district had
been, for the most part, early enclosed, and were now
swamped by the tide of buildings. Newton Heath, a
common or waste of 140 acres which survived through
the eighteenth century, was enclosed in 1802. No provision was made on its enclosure for any recreation, but
a liberal allotment was made in aid of the Poor Rates.
"At present," wrote Dr. J. P. Kay in 1833, "the entire
labouring population of Manchester is without any sea-
son of recreation, and is ignorant of all amusements,
excepting that very small portion which frequents the
theatre. Healthful exercise in the open air is seldom
or never taken by the artisans of this town, and their
health certainly suffers considerable depression from this
deprivation. One reason of this state of the people is,
that all scenes of interest are remote from the town, and
that the walks which can be enjoyed by the poor are
chiefly the turnpike roads, alternately dusty or muddy.
Were parks provided, recreation would be taken with

avidity, and one of the first results would be a better use of the Sunday, and a substitution of innocent amusement at all other times, for the debasing pleasures now in vogue. I need not inform you how sad is our labouring population here." Ten years later the position was unchanged. "With a teeming population," wrote Mr. Mott, "literally overflowing her boundaries, she has no public walks or resorts, either for the youthful or the adult portion of the community to snatch an hour's enjoyment." On one occasion, and one only, such institutional gardens as existed were opened to this melancholy population: "On the holiday given at Manchester in celebration of Her Majesty's marriage, extensive arrangements were made for holding a Chartist meeting, and for getting up what was called a demonstration of the working classes, which greatly alarmed the municipal magistrates. Sir Charles Shaw, the Chief Commissioner of Police, induced the mayor to get the Botanical Gardens, Zoological Gardens, and Museum of that town, and other institutions thrown open to the working classes at the hour they were urgently invited to attend the Chartist meeting. The mayor undertook to be personally answerable for any damage that occurred from throwing open the gardens and other institutions to the classes who had never before entered them. The effect was that not more than two or three hundred attended the political meeting, which entirely failed, and scarcely five shillings' worth of damage was done in the gardens or in the public institutions by the workpeople, who were highly pleased. A further effect produced was, that the charges before the police of drunkenness and riot were on that day less than the average of cases on ordinary days."

Attempts were made from time to time in the House of Commons to save some common opportunities for enjoyment. Perhaps the most interesting was Peel's attempt to amend the Municipal Corporations Bill in Committee in 1835. In many towns there were common lands over which the privileged class of freemen had legal rights, which the public in some cases could use for recreation. When the Whigs brought in their measure for reforming the government of towns, Peel obtained the insertion of a clause which, had it survived, might have made considerable difference to the disposal of these lands.

Peel's view was "that most of the property of corporations was intended for the benefit of the community at large, and it would be desirable that the community should recover it as soon as possible." By long prescription it had been appropriated to the use of certain descriptions of inhabitants only, and it was now desirable that it should be put "into the hands of the commonalty as speedily as possible consistent with justice to the rights of individuals." The Whigs accepted Peel's view; but the House of Lords took out of the Bill the clauses that gave effect to it. The House of Commons was unhappily so much occupied with fighting the Lords on other points, that it accepted defeat on this.

That public interest had been aroused, owing no doubt to the findings of the 1833 Committee, was also shown when in 1836 a Bill to make easier the Enclosure of Common Fields came up for discussion in the Commons. A clause was inserted giving a radius round towns in which no enclosure of common fields under the Act was permitted. The radius varied from one mile for a town of 5,000 inhabitants to three miles for 100,000 and ten miles for London. These provisions did not apply to wastes or commons, as they were not included in the Act.

The next move for the defence of public rights was made by Hume. On March 9, 1837, he proposed a resolution in the House of Commons "that in all Inclosure Bills provision be made for leaving an open space sufficient for the purposes of exercise and recreation of the neighbouring population." Peel, then leader of the Opposition, though doubtful about the actual form of the resolution, gave warm support to Hume's object. He pointed out, with truth, that the subject had been urged on the attention of the Legislature, but that the Legislature had refused to attend. He laid down a sound doctrine that though the people might have no legal right to portions of waste lands or commons "they had a moral right," and he urged that even where no enclosure took place it would be a "wise and prudent expenditure of public money" to give a grant of £5,000 or £10,000 to aid local authorities.

Hume's motion was passed. It was supplemented two years later by Harvey, who moved (April 9, 1830) a resolution, afterwards made into a standing order, that in all Enclosure Bills "provision be made for leaving an open space in the most appropriate situation sufficient for purposes of exercise and recreation of the neighbouring population," and that provision be made "for efficient fencing of the allotment." Harvey made a long speech about the iniquities of Enclosure Bills, and the small allowance made for recreation allotments, instancing cases where three acres had been allotted out of 1,300, or 10 to 20 out of 10,000. He suggested that there should be "a poor man's Commissioner" to see that a suitable reservation was made, and urged the House to protect the poor in view of the "spirit of the times and the symptoms moving around them."

The intentions of the House of Commons were good, but the actual allotments made under these standing orders were meagre. An illustration is afforded by the case of Bradford in Yorkshire. Near Bradford there was an open space of from 20 to 30 acres called Fairweather Green. According to a witness before the 1840 Health of Towns Committee, this space was used for games by "the population for five and six miles round; it is the only place for the purpose in the whole neighbourhood." But whilst this Committee was sitting, a private Bill was passing through Parliament, prepared by Mr. Lister, one of the largest proprietors concerned, to enclose this

green and some other parcels of waste land, amounting
in all to 170 acres. Mr. Joseph Ellison, the witness referred to, protested against the reservation in the Act of
three acres only "as a Place of Exercise and Recreation
for the neighbouring Population," a population that he
estimated at 120,000. On Fairweather Green, he pointed
out, it was the custom to play at cricket, and "a game
we call spell and nur; they will drive a ball, 10, 11, 12,
13, and 14 score; they cannot play at those games in
three acres."

When considering the small size of the recreation allotments, we must remember that a tiny playground, combined with a fairly broad walk, was all that most
members of Parliament thought necessary for the working classes. Roebuck was almost the only speaker who
saw the need for bigger spaces. "On the commons, the
sports of the village took place. (Laughter.) They might
laugh if they liked; he considered this to be a point of
much importance. He liked that the poor should have
the right of going on the commons with their wives and
families; he liked to go himself among the furze bushes,
and he did not wish to take away what he enjoyed himself from them. . . ." When reminded by another
speaker that already in all Enclosure Bills "a portion
of land for the exercise of the poor" was set aside, Roebuck retorted: "Yes, a small space; I am for a large
common."

A study of the local papers shows how great a strain
a life without playing-fields or amenities of any kind put
upon the English temperament. Towns pass laws to
forbid children from playing with tops in the streets;
correspondents write to complain of the flying of kites,
and magistrates impose severe fines on men and boys
for running races on the turnpike roads, on the ground
that this practice has become a general nuisance.

There was another use of land that was of great value
to inhabitants of towns. To indoor workers gardening
can be an amusement. The system of allotments for

growing vegetables, said a Committee on the subject in 1843, "partly supplies that deficiency of innocent amusement and rational recreation which weighs so particularly upon the lower classes of this country." But though allotments were usually successful when tried, there were few districts where the supply equalled the demand. The main reason seems to have been that though a fair number of landowners were willing to let their land in this way, the business of collecting the rents and dealing with a large number of tenants made the system unpopular with land agents. In some parts of the Midlands this difficulty was overcome by a Labourers' Friend Society, with 63 branches, which dealt direct with the landowner and paid the rents in a lump sum. It might seem at first sight that enclosure would afford a good opportunity for making such allotments, for when land was enclosed other considerations were thrust aside in the interests of increased cultivation. But spade cultivation counted for little on these occasions. The objection was put bluntly before the 1844 Committee on Inclosure: the more you took for allotments, the less there was to be divided up among the various proprietors. Near towns, land was of course more valuable, so this objection operated there even more strongly. Lord Ashley (afterwards Lord Shaftesbury) and William Cowper (afterwards Lord Mount Temple) both made valiant attempts in Parliament to help the increase of allotments by introducing special Bills for the purpose, but with no success. The only result of the Allotments agitation, so far as parliamentary action was concerned, was a meagre clause in the General Enclosure Act of 1845.

We have seen that during the thirties there was considerable concern in Parliament for the loss of public rights by enclosure. Yet in 1845 Parliament passed the General Enclosure Act, making it easier to convert land that was still available for the public enjoyment into private property. Legally, as we have seen, the public had no claim to use or to wander over this land; practically they were not, and could not, be kept out. To obtain the full benefit of what the law said belonged to them, and to them alone, to shut up the land and shut others out, the lord of the soil and the owners of common rights had to gain in each case the consent of Parliament. The 1845 Act revolutionized, quickened, and cheapened the whole process. Instead of each enclosure requiring its own separate machinery, a permanent department was now set up with three Commissioners who were empowered to carry out the Act. The expenses were no longer provided entirely by the enclosers, for the department was supported out of public funds. What had become of the concern of the thirties? Why was Parliament so ready to acquiesce in making it easy to close up vast tracts of land that had lain open from time immemorial? Population was increasing rapidly, means of transport were increasing rapidly, and people were moving about outside towns. It would seem reasonable to expect that Parliament would be not less but more concerned in the forties than in the thirties.

The answer, which can only be dealt with shortly here, is to be found in the peculiar circumstances of agriculture, combined with a disastrous confidence in fallacious statistics. The period of high farming was beginning; the researches of the great German chemist Liebig opened out new vistas of improvement; artificial manures, guano, rape dust, etc., were introduced, new systems of drainage were discussed, new machinery came into use. The new science of agriculture seemed to promise that wilderness and wastes would blossom when money had been spent on them, and money would only be found under private ownership. Hence, it was all-important to cheapen enclosure. The matter was made more urgent by an ingenious calculation about the amount of waste land lying ready for the application of artificial manures. A parliamentary return in 1843 gave an estimate of the amount of common or waste land in parishes where tithes had been commuted. If the same proportion held good for the rest of England and Wales, you had some 8,000,000 acres, and adding to that a rough estimate of 2,000,000 acres of common fields, you had the gratifying, if somewhat surprising, total of 10,000,000 acres out of some 37,000,000 acres awaiting improvement. A parliamentary return 20 years later, made with rather more care, though it too was subjected to charges of exaggeration, made the total some 3,250,000 instead of 10,000,000. But at the time the statisticians were unchallenged, and to those living in the hungry forties, the 10,000,000 acres opened up a vast prospect. The anti-Corn-Law campaign made the whole question vital. Repealers, however anxious for importation, could hardly oppose a measure to increase home-grown supplies, while anti-repealers saw here an answer to the agitation. Instead of allowing foreign wheat to enter free, turn those 60,000 acres of Surrey commons, and those wide Welsh and Yorkshire moors, and that great stretch of hills that run from Derby up into Scotland, into prairies of waving corn, tended by prosperous, industrious, and virtuous labourers. Nothing seemed impossible with the growth of scientific agriculture.

The prevailing optimism was well expressed by Lord Palmerston (House of Commons, July 4, 1845). "In England and Wales there were about 37,000,000 acres, and it was calculated that of these 37,000,000 acres 10,000,000 would come under the operation of the present Bill, and it was in evidence before the committee that setting aside the temporary employment which would be given in their enclosure, and in drainage, tilling, and in erecting those buildings which would be consequent on enclosure, the permanent additional employment given to the labouring classes might be stated at one labourer and his family for every 50 acres; so that if this calculation were applied to the 10,000,000 acres,

there would be given by their enclosure additional employment to 200,000 agricultural families.''

Later generations may well be thankful that Palmerston's dream did not come true, and that the heaths and
moors proved less amenable to treatment than was expected. But much mischief had been done, and, however much one can explain it, it remains a curious fact
that such an Act should have been passed with so little
opposition at a time when the movement for public
parks was growing in strength. The explanation seems
to be the widespread impression that ample precautions
had been taken to protect public interests. These included, it may be noted, a few years later, a provision
that parliamentary sanction must be given to all enclosures. *The Times* alone saw the real state of affairs
and fought a valiant battle, but its warnings fell on
deaf ears. The next twenty years afford a melancholy
picture of the disregard of public interests by a department well-intentioned, but deficient in imagination and
foresight and untouched by any criticism. Year after
year the Inclosure Commissioners presented their Report, and followed up the Report with an Annual Bill
which was passed as a matter of routine without discussion. A false sense of security had engendered apathy
in place of those spasmodic and occasionally effectual
protests evoked by the more flagrant earlier abuses.
Parliament trusted to the Commissioners, the Commissioners trusted to Parliament to protect public interests. In 1862, for the first time after the passing of the
1845 Act, Parliament intervened and made an alteration
in the Annual Inclosure Bill, in the case of Chigwell, by
substituting 50 acres for the 5 acres of recreation allotment allowed by the Commission, but it was not till
1865 that public interest was effectively roused. With
the formation of the Commons Preservation Society and
the action of Eversley, Fawcett and many others, a
new era begins. But the story of that long struggle does
not come into this book.

CHAPTER VII

THE NEW POOR LAW

"In a community such as now exists in this country, so largely occupied in commercial industry, and liable to be affected by the changes continually taking place in trades and manufactures, there must be alternations of prosperity and adversity, of activity and stagnation, of the demand for labour exceeding the supply, and of the supply exceeding the demand; and such changes will necessarily have the effect of occasionally throwing able-bodied persons out of employment. But this is a contingency against which men may provide by the exercise of care and forethought. They can, however, hardly be expected to do so, if on the occurrence of every reverse they are permitted to fall back upon the poor rates for unconditional relief; and the condition of the relief being given in the workhouse is therefore as necessary for the protection of the rate-payers, as the relief itself is necessary for those who without it might be subjected to the extremity of want."—Sir George Nicholls, *one of the Poor Law Commissioners, in* History of the English Poor Law, *New Edition,* 1890, *vol.* 2, *p.* 427.

DISRAELI said of the Poor Law of 1834 that it was impossible "to conceive a revolution which exercised a greater influence upon the people at large. . . . If they had not, in passing the Poor Law, outraged the constitution or violated the law, they had done that which he conceived was of greater importance; they had outraged the manners of the people." How far was Disraeli's description of the new Poor Law correct?

If the historian of our age turns to the publications of the International Labour Office for light on our social life, he will find that certain arrangements are common

to most European countries, designed to prevent or
alleviate poverty, sickness, and misfortune. If he takes
one of the more advanced nations, he will find Trade
Boards, Unemployment Insurance, Old Age Pensions,
Widows' Pensions, special treatment for underfed children, special provision for insanity and other diseases,
special arrangements for medical services. In some countries he will find all of these institutions, in all he will
find some. If he turns to English life between 1800 and
1850 he will find, so far as the State is concerned, one
single institution in use for the treatment of all these
problems: the Poor Law. This was true before the revolution of 1834: it was true after that revolution. What,
then, was done by that revolution; how did it outrage
the manners of the English people? To answer that
question we must put the revolution against its historical
background.

The escaped convict in Mr. Galsworthy's play reminds
the parson, when he is found taking refuge in the vestry,
that the Church was once the sanctuary for fugitives.
In England in the Middle Ages, as on the Continent of
Europe, the Church took care, so far as care was taken,
of the destitute and the sick. The parish was the unit
for these purposes. The cost was borne partly by alms,
partly by parish property (parishes had property in different forms, sometimes in the form of an inn), partly by
the proceeds of convivial entertainment known as
Church Ales, and later by Church Rates. In the sixteenth century, as a result of a movement for reform, not peculiar to England, nor originating in
England, for the chief name in its history is that
of Vives, the State began to accept responsibility
for the problem that had hitherto been thrown upon the
Church. A number of Acts of Parliament, beginning
with a modest Act in 1536 and culminating with the
famous Act of 1601, made provision for the relief of the
destitute. The justices were directed to see that every
parish had a stock of wool, hemp, and other things, in

order to provide employment; recalcitrants were to be committed to a house of correction, householders were to be compelled to contribute. This legislation was followed by half a century of remarkable activity, the Privy Council putting strong pressure upon the local authorities to carry out constructive schemes.

This short spell of centralised effort was followed by a long spell of local autonomy. Parliament stiffened the restrictions of Settlement Laws and Vagrancy Acts, but the administration of the Poor Law was left to local effort guided by Acts of Parliament. The Acts that concern our study are those of 1722, 1782, and 1796.

At the beginning of the eighteenth century the man or woman needing help could apply to an overseer who was an unpaid officer, or to a magistrate. He might be given help at home, or he might be relieved in the workhouse. In 1722 Parliament, anxious to make administration stricter, encouraged the building of workhouses, authorizing parishes to build workhouses without a special Act of Parliament and enacting that anyone who refused to enter a workhouse forfeited any claim to relief. This Act made the law more stringent. In 1782 a reformer named Gilbert carried an Act which in some respects made administration more indulgent. Parishes adopting his Act, known as Gilbert's Act, could make special arrangements. In these parishes, grouped in incorporations, the workhouse was to be reserved for children and the aged and infirm; the able-bodied were to be given employment outside the workhouse, or, failing employment, were to be given relief.

This was the state of the law when the French war broke out. There were a number of parishes in which the able-bodied were either employed or relieved in their homes by the parish, the workhouse being the refuge for special classes, and others where a person refusing help inside the workhouse lost his right to relief. The French war produced a crisis in which this system broke down. For in 1795 high prices created a position so desperate that it was universally recognized that something must be done for the agricultural labourer whose wages no longer maintained him. Arthur Young came forward with a proposal for the regulation of wages, and he was supported by Whitbread and Fox. Whitbread introduced two Bills for this purpose in 1795 and 1800, but Pitt threw his great influence against them and this plan was rejected. The method of relief adopted, that of making up wages out of the rates, has become famous in history as the Speenhamland system, for it was at Speenhamland that the country gentlemen of Berkshire met and drew up a scale of wages fluctuating with the price of bread, based on the size of a man's family, that was generally observed in other parts of England. The same year Parliament, acting in this spirit, passed a Bill introduced by Sir William Young, relaxing the restrictions of the Act of 1722 and sanctioning and encouraging outdoor relief.*

To understand the full effect of the Speenhamland plan of making up wages out of the rates, we must remember that it was soon mixed up with the Gilbert plan for public employment. One method for dealing with applicants for relief was to hire them out to the farmers in turn, the parish paying two-thirds of their wages, the farmer the other third. In some cases these labourers were put up for public auction every Saturday night. The Poor Law soon became a vicious circle from which the poor man could not escape. Where things were at their worst a man who had any savings could not get help from the rates: a man who did not get help from the rates could not get a farmer to employ him.

When the Royal Commission in 1833 examined the problem of Poor Relief, they discovered a number of abuses, but the abuse that stood out in their minds as the main cause of degradation and extravagance was

* 36 George III, c. 23.

the Speenhamland plan. The Commissioners, therefore,
recommended the extinction of this system and a return
to the stricter ideas of 1722. So drastic a change could
not be carried out at once, if at all, by local authorities
accustomed to the old habits and amenable to local
influences. It was therefore proposed to set up a central
authority with exceptional powers and to reorganize local
administration by combining parishes into unions, with
Boards of Guardians elected for the whole district. The
nation, that is, was to return to the method of the seventeenth century, when pressure was put upon the local
authorities from the centre.

Lord Grey's Government introduced a Bill in 1834
to give effect to this report. The Bill contained 110 sections, but it did not attack in detail the evils exposed by
the Commission. Instead, it created a central department
consisting of three paid Commissioners with a paid
Secretary, with power to make regulations and orders.
The administration of the relief of the poor was to be
put under the control of this Commission. The alarm
excited by the abuses and burdens of the Speenhamland
system was such that the Bill passed its second reading
by 319 votes to 20. There was great opposition in the
Press from the first, ranging from *The Times* to the
Political Register, and certain of its proposals were
fiercely attacked in Parliament, but the Bill became law
in August of that year. Some Ministers were afraid that
so drastic a measure might lead to an outbreak of violence, and Melbourne disliked giving a new authority
power to issue mandatory orders without the sanction
of the Secretary of State. But Nassau Senior, the famous
economist, the ablest member of the Poor Law Inquiry
Commission, who had great influence with members of
the Cabinet, persuaded them that no methods less rigorous would meet the public need. So Ministers held on
their course. But it is significant that whereas the second
reading passed by 319 votes to 20, the third reading
passed by 187 to 50.

Several members of Grey's Cabinet had been afraid that
if the Act were put into force in the agricultural districts
it would lead to another outbreak of Swing riots. But
this did not happen. The passing of the Act was followed by three very good harvests, and the rapid development of railway construction at the time eased the
immediate difficulties of the transition. Wages rose a
little, and though there were riots of a kind in East
Kent, Chesham, and Bedfordshire, they were quickly
suppressed. In the South, consequently, the Commissioners made rapid progress.

When the Commissioners turned to the North they
found a different state of things. The effect of the Speenhamland system in the South had been to demoralize
completely the conditions of employment, to spread
pauperism far and wide, and to turn the agricultural
labourer in many parishes into a kind of public serf.
When it was abolished considerable suffering was
caused, but most labourers found employment either on
the farms or on the railways. The Speenhamland system
was in force to some extent in the North, for outdoor
relief was given in the industrial districts to some of the
hand-loom weavers, a class by this time permanently
underpaid, dying a lingering death. The Assistant Commissioner, Gilbert Henderson, who reported on Lancashire, argued that there were important differences
between the case of the hand-loom weaver and that of
the agricultural labourer. The hand-loom weaver was a
pieceworker, and the overseer could calculate what he
ought to earn. The Allowance System in the opinion of
the Assistant Commissioner had the effect, not of making
the hand-loom weaver relax his efforts, but of stimulating him beyond his strength. At Oldham the hand-loom
weavers were reluctant to apply for relief, and were only
driven to it when they had three or four children under
ten.

The Poor Law Commissioners themselves, reviewing
their policy in 1847, drew a distinction between North

and South. "They have considered the main object of
the Legislature in passing the Poor Law Amendment
Act to have been the extinction of the Allowance System,
or the system of making up the wages of the labourers
out of the poor's rate. With this view their regulations
respecting the limitation of outdoor relief have been
almost exclusively confined to the able-bodied in health;
and these regulations have been issued particularly to
the rural Unions, inasmuch as it was in the agricultural
counties and not in the large towns of manufacturing
districts that the Allowance System was most prevalent
and led to the most dangerous consequences. It is significant that even staunch friends to the principle of the
new Poor Law were not prepared to extinguish the practice of giving outdoor relief to hand-loom weavers. "In
the Union with which he was connected," said Sir James
Graham in the House of Commons, "there was a large
body of hand-loom weavers, and he did not hesitate to
say, during the last winter it would have been utterly
impossible to have conducted the affairs of that Union
without relief, though sparingly administered, and with
great caution, to the able-bodied labourer."

There was another class of able-bodied workmen receiving relief from time to time in large numbers from
the rates. The industrial districts were liable to mass unemployment, a form of unemployment which was unknown in the southern counties. Edward Baines, the
member for Leeds, like Graham a strong supporter in
general of the new Poor Law, called attention to this
difficulty. "Circumstances occasionally occurred there
which threw 400 or 500 persons in a single parish out
of employment. In such cases could they enforce the
rule; or were they prepared to build enough workhouses
to carry it out?" In these cases the granting of outdoor
relief had clearly not entailed the consequences of personal degradation which had followed in the South,
when parishes faced with their growing difficulties had
so managed the Allowance System as to put a moral

stigma upon the great body of agricultural labourers.
The southern labourer had lost his status before the
revolution in the Poor Law. But the poor man in the
North, who had received poor relief in his home as a
hand-loom weaver or as an unemployed workman, had
not been under that stigma. He now found himself
threatened with the punishment of the workhouse. Even
men who had deep sympathy with the lot of the agricultural labourer believed that the new Poor Law, drastic as it was, was an improvement on the terrible
conditions created in the villages by the abuses of the
old. No person with such sympathies in the North could
think with patience of punishing great masses of unemployed workmen, victims of the new industrial system,
with the rigours that were meant for incorrigible idlers.
It is easy, then, to understand that the threat of the
Bastille, as the workhouse was called, provoked in the
North a storm of indignation which prevented the Commissioners from repeating the success they had achieved
in the South. The *West Riding Herald* could boast, in
July 1837, that "the new Poor Law has been suspended
in the West Riding through the sturdy resistance of the
people."

The new Poor Law had many enemies besides the
poor: clergymen angry over the new Marriage Registra-
tion Act which had been hitched on to the Poor Law;
country gentlemen who disliked taking orders from
Whitehall; tradesmen who lost sources of profit, and
good Party men, who saw an excellent opportunity for
heaping odium on a Government they hated. There were
others, again, who acted from larger motives, country
gentlemen, parsons, doctors, professional men, and
manufacturers, who thought the new law harsh and
unjust and took an active part in agitating against it
on these grounds.

This resistance took various forms. Public meetings
were held in the chief towns of the West Riding and
South Lancashire, and organizations for obstructing the

question. He had presided over a Committee on
labourers' wages in 1824. The evidence submitted to
that Committee of the evils that had followed the
Allowance System had made such an impression on him
that he never could give any attention to any other
aspect of the problem. The attacks from which he defended the Commission were led in the House of
Commons by John Walter, editor of *The Times*, Thomas
Wakley, editor of *The Lancet*, and John Fielden, the
great factory reformer. In 1837 Disraeli entered Parliament, and from that time his biting tongue was at their
service. These men did invaluable work, bringing abuses
to light, and checking some of the cruelties of the new
system. Thus in the House the Opposition was that of
free-lances, but it represented a great body of opinion
in the country where Conservative sentiment was much
more hostile both to the Act and to the Commission than
the Conservative Party in the House of Commons.
The Conservative papers in Leeds, Halifax, Wakefield,
Liverpool, Bolton, and other northern towns used language on this question as vehement as anything said or
written by the Chartists. During the General Election
of 1837 which followed the death of William IV this
hostility found fierce expression. One of the Conservative candidates at Bradford described the new Poor Law
as "that Bill which separated those whom God had
joined together, gave a premium to murder, made
poverty a crime, starved the poor man and tried to
prove whether he could not live upon bread and water."
Beckett, the Conservative candidate at Leeds, said he
had done his utmost to prevent the introduction of the
Act into the West Riding, and Stuart Wortley, one of
the Conservative candidates for the West Riding, stood
as an opponent of the Poor Law. Reminded that Peel
and Wellington had supported the Bill of 1834, these
candidates replied that they were not bound by anything that their leaders had said, and Stuart Wortley
argued that the Commissioners were worse than the Act.

Even so orthodox a Liberal candidate as Lord Morpeth spoke in his election address to the West Riding of the necessity of compromise, and one of the Liberal candidates for Bradford declared: "What is good in the measure I will keep, what is bad I will exterminate."

Politicians are often more violent in their views when their Party is in opposition. In 1841 the Conservatives took office. Peel, the new Prime Minister, treated the angry sentiment of his Party with characteristic independence. The hated Commission was prolonged first for six months, and then for five years. Fielden took the opportunity to ask for a Committee of Inquiry on the specific question of the influence of the new Poor Law on wages. The Government resisted the proposal, and Fielden was only supported by eight members, a distinguished little group, for it included both Cobden and Disraeli. A Conservative member, Escott, raised a fundamental issue, for he moved to insert in the Bill, which was to prolong the life of the Commission, the following clause: "That it shall be lawful for all Boards of Guardians of the poor in England and Wales to grant such relief as in their judgment shall be necessary to poor persons at their own homes, any order, rule, or regulation of the Poor Law Commissioners notwithstanding." Escott admitted that this would open the door again to the Allowance System, and he was defeated by 90 to 55. Graham, in reply, argued that the figures which he gave, revealing the large increase in the volume of outdoor relief, showed that ample discretion was given to the local authorities in practice. But in 1844 the Government amended the law in some important respects, removing one great cause of discontent by dissociating from the Poor Law all legal questions relating to bastardy. At the same time, the administration of the law was relaxed, Chadwick having happily been diverted to more suitable tasks. In 1845, however, a storm broke which did more damage to the Poor Law Commission than any of the previous agitations.

One of the forms of task work imposed in certain workhouses was the crushing of bones, and the master of the Andover Workhouse was accused of starving the paupers so that they fought among themselves for the gristle and marrow to be found in the half-putrid bones given to them for this purpose. Indignation led to a demand for inquiry, so vehement and general that the Government had to yield, and the revelations that followed made a profound impression on the public mind. For an inquiry that began with the Andover scandals ended as an inquisition into the life and methods of the Poor Law Commission. When asked for a Committee on the Andover Workhouse, Graham, who made a bad start, regretting the time Parliament was spending on "a workhouse squabble," felt himself obliged to give way to the insistence of the House of Commons. It was then proposed to extend the inquiry to the conduct of the Poor Law Commissioners. The Government resisted, but the motion was carried by 92 votes to 69. The Committee was set up, and it was soon deep in the domestic quarrels of the Poor Law Commission. Frankland Lewis, no longer a Commissioner, spoke of his perpetual troubles with the secretary, "as unscrupulous and as dangerous an officer as ever I saw within the walls of an office." Chadwick made it clear that in this uncongenial partnership there was about as much confidence on one side of the table as on the other. As Commissioners and Secretary had friends on the Committee, and as there were members who were glad enough to bring the Commission into discredit by pressing for disclosures, these recriminations let a great deal of unkind daylight into the past. They settled the fate of a body which, obnoxious already for its public transactions, was now mistrusted for transactions that had hitherto been private. Decisions that were unpopular did not gain in respect when it was known by what methods and in what kind of atmosphere they had been reached. The Committee, after condemning the administration of the law in the Andover Union, passed on Disraeli's initiative, by eight votes to four, a sweeping condemnation. "On a review of the proceedings of the Commissioners with respect to the Andover Inquiries and towards Mr. Parker and Mr. Day, the Committee are of opinion that their conduct has been irregular and arbitrary, not in accordance with the statute under which they exercise their functions, and such as to shake public confidence in the administration of the law."

Whatever might have been made, under different conditions, of an experiment in centralized administration by a body without a parliamentary head, it was clear that this particular experiment could be continued no longer. The Whigs came back to power in 1847, and Sir George Grey, the new Home Secretary, carried an Act setting up a new Poor Law Board in place of the Poor Law Commission. The new Board consisted nominally of the Lord President of the Council, the Lord Privy Seal, the Home Secretary, and the Chancellor of the Exchequer, together with the President, who was to be eligible to sit in Parliament, and two paid Secretaries, of whom one was also to be eligible to sit in Parliament. The Act also contained provisions making the administration of the Poor Law more humane.

These changes did not, of course, reconcile the working classes to the new Poor Law. The Commission had gone, but the law remained. The law was administered by Guardians with a property qualification, elected by a system of voting which virtually excluded the wage-earning classes, that lasted until 1894. The 25,000 Guardians were mostly farmers and retail tradesmen, and the complaint of want of sympathy and consideration continued for half a century. It might seem that the poor had gained very little by the change. Yet the Poor Law never again became the object of an agitation so violent and widespread.

To understand the episode of English history that began when Chadwick became Secretary of the Commission, and ended when the new Poor Law Board undertook the administration of the less rigid law, we must remember that between 1834 and 1847 every workman saw himself exposed to the danger of imprisonment in the Bastille, with the break-up of his family and home at the dictation of the Poor Law Commissioners. That is how the struggle appeared to the working-class mind. The Poor Law Commissioners stood for an alien power, inaccessible to pity or justice. In this struggle rumour flew from place to place, and local incidents were known from one end of the country to the other. In the eighteenth century, brutalities in a particular workhouse were not heard of outside the district; in the nineteenth century, any workman in Bradford or Gateshead could tell you that a man had died in Eton Workhouse, who had not been allowed to see his wife alone, and that the Preston Guardians were debating whether or not a bell should be tolled at paupers' funerals. The Press was a new propagandist force. The Conservative papers filled their columns with cases of hardship, and speakers like Parson Bull were reckless in bringing charges against the Commissioners and their subordinates on hearsay evidence. Much was happening that deserved to be exposed and blamed, but in such an agitation it happens inevitably that the truth, bad as it is, becomes worse in the telling. The tone and language of the Commissioners embittered the struggle, and Peel protested strongly in the House of Commons against the indifference they displayed to the feelings of the poorer classes. The working-class world was reminded every day, in the Press, on the platform, and in official documents, that the only choice for the poor man, when misfortune befell him, was the choice between starvation and disgrace. To understand how deep and vivid was this impression, we must turn to the workhouse.

The mixed workhouse of the eighteenth century has been described by Crabbe in a famous picture:

> "There Children dwell who know no parents' care:
> Parents, who know no Children's love, dwell there;
> Heart-broken Matrons on their joyless bed,
> Forsaken Wives and Mothers never wed;
> Dejected Widows with unheeded tears,
> And crippled Age with more than childhood's fears;
> The Lame, the Blind, and, far the happiest they!
> The moping Idiot and the Madman gay."

The Commissioners who inquired into the Poor Laws in 1833 wished to put an end to the mixed workhouse. Nassau Senior and Bishop Blomfield were specially anxious to isolate the children; others to isolate the aged. Chadwick, who pressed this policy, argued that in this way the old could enjoy their comforts, the children receive education, and the able-bodied be subjected to necessary discipline. Unfortunately, Chadwick's good advice made less impression that his bad. The Poor Law Commissioners kept the mixed workhouse and, in improving it, turned it more definitely and grimly into a prison. Disraeli said in 1841 that no other term than that of imprisonment could be given to the confinement which the poor underwent in the Union workhouse.

The Union workhouse was, of course, much larger than the old Parish workhouse. The larger the workhouse, the more detailed and exact the regulations that are necessary to keep order and arrangement. In this case these regulations proceeded from a central authority setting up, or seeking to set up, a system of discipline to be imposed upon Union workhouses all over the country. The Commissioners began by laying down the most rigorous rules. From 1836 to 1842 silence was prescribed at all meals, a rule of which Wakley remarked that the silent system was generally regarded as the most severe form of punishment in prison life; and paupers could not see their friends except in the presence of Master, Matron, or porter. Playing at cards was forbidden. Such discipline could make no allowance for the circumstances of a particular workhouse, a particular class, or a particular pauper. It is easy to imagine what this iron discipline looked like to the poor of the West Riding, when they learned that the Dewsbury Guardians had wished to allow an old man to smoke a pipe, but were warned that they would first have to get the leave of the Poor Law Commissioners.

A lawyer, writing in 1852, said that he had visited many prisons and lunatic asylums, not only in England, but in France and Germany. "A single English workhouse," he went on to say, "contains more that justly calls for condemnation in the principle on which it is established than is found in the very worst prisons or public lunatic asylums that I have seen. The workhouse as now organized is a reproach and disgrace peculiar to England: nothing corresponding to it is to be found throughout the whole continent of Europe." The explanation is simple. There were collected in the workhouse young and old, sick and mad, vagrants passing a night, and crippled old men and women who could never hope to leave it, the victims of misfortune and the victims of vice. "It passed the wit of man," as Mr. and Mrs. Webb well put it, "to contrive a General Mixed Workhouse that should appear so uncomfortable as to deter from entrance every person who could possibly earn a bare living wage; and yet be, in fact, so endurable, and withal, so improving, to those who could not possibly maintain themselves by work, as to induce them both to enter and voluntarily to remain for as long as was socially expedient." It would have been difficult in any case to make the workhouse a terror to the idle and vicious, and a comfort to the sick and unfortunate. But in the minds of the Commissioners the workhouse was meant to be a deterrent institution for all sorts and conditions of the poor. "With regard to the aged and infirm," they wrote in 1840, "there is a

strong disposition on the part of a portion of the public
so to modify the arrangements of these establishments
as to place them on the footing of almshouses. The consequences which would flow from this change have only
to be pointed out to show its inexpediency and its danger.
If the condition of the inmates of a workhouse were to
be so regulated as to invite the aged and infirm of the
labouring classes to take refuge in it, it would immediately be useless as a test between indigence and in-
dolence or fraud." This idea, that vice and idleness
were to be discouraged by punishing the sick and the
unfortunate, was carried so far that the Commissioners
would not help to educate pauper children living on
outdoor relief. Chadwick wanted to have a training
establishment for all children who came under the control of the Guardians, but the Commissioners were so
afraid of taking the sting out of pauperism that they
would not even allow the Guardians to pay the school
fee of twopence a week for the children maintained on
outdoor relief.

The Commissioners kept the mixed workhouse, but
they classified the inmates, forbidding any communication
between the different classes. In this way husbands and
wives, parents and children, were kept rigorously apart.
Before 1834 the practice of workhouses varied. In some
of the Lancashire workhouses, such as those at Liverpool, Oldham, and Wigan, married couples were not
separated. At Manchester, on the other hand, they were
always separated. "A case occurred where an old man
of eighty, a tinker, who, though in great distress, turned
back from the house when he found that he must be
separated from his wife, an old woman of seventy.
He was afterwards, however, compelled by want to
take refuge in the house, and died there after remain-
ing some time, according to the rule, deprived of his
wife's society." The Commissioners made a strict rule
for all cases, and this rule was denounced again and
again in the House of Commons by Walter and other

critics of the Poor Law. The Commissioners defended
their decision in a characteristic passage in their First
Report. "Under these circumstances, we cannot admit
that the charge of undue severity attaches to the continued and more complete enforcement of the rule for
the separation of the sexes during the temporary resid-
ence in the workhouse, as a condition of being relieved
from the danger of perishing for want." This feature of
workhouse life inspired many passionate speeches. An
address from Newcastle women spoke of the Poor Law
as separating those whom God had joined together.
The Commissioners had to make concessions, and in
1847 Parliament passed an Act forbidding the separation of married people over sixty.

Peel and Graham both complained of the want of
sympathy and feeling which the Commissioners exhibited in their public documents. One illustration shows
vividly how little Chadwick, so admirable in his ex-
posure of abuses, was able to understand human nature
when he was called on to administer a policy. If one
thing stands out in the records of the minds and feelings
of the poor in history, it is the passionate concern for
the treatment of the body after death. The inscriptions
that tell us of proletarian life in the Roman Empire
show that the mean and the miserable alike in the days
before and the days after the introduction of Christianity clung to the hope that their friends would pay
some tribute to their memory. The burial club is an
institution so old and so common in the life of Europe
that one might suppose that the fear of being thrown
on one side as a nameless carcase after death has
troubled and haunted the mind of man more persistently
than the fear of sickness or starvation.

Chadwick trod on this universal sentiment as if all
life had gone from it. The last touch of degradation was
added to the lot of the pauper when, in response to a
circular which he issued in March 1836, the Guardians
in certain Unions decided that the bell should not be

tolled at pauper funerals. Walter read a letter to the
House of Commons from the Mayor of Morpeth stating
that two men had been driven to suicide by the barbari-
ties of the Poor Law. The Mayor went on to say that
the Board of Guardians for the same Union (a Union
embracing sixty or seventy townships) had only a few
days before resolved that the common decencies of
burial should not be observed as heretofore towards
deceased paupers. The Rector of Bishop's Waltham, in
criticizing the new Poor Law before the Select Committee in 1837, remarked: "The mode of burying the
poor, separation from their friends in death, the decent
rites of interment not being provided, even the funeral
bell not being tolled—all these things are an outrage
upon the feelings of the poor." Chadwick in this was
overruled by the Commissioners. In a circular to the
Guardians of March 1, 1836, he had included amongst
the charges commonly found in overseers' accounts, but
not authorized by any statute, charges for tolling bells
at paupers' funerals. This letter went to every Union in
the country, and it was clear from evidence taken by
the Select Committee of 1837 that some Unions acted
upon it. Frankland Lewis, however, intervened, and a
corrected circular was sent out a month later in which
the word "excessive" was inserted before the charges
for tolling. Chadwick prevaricated when pressed on this
point by Walter, and it was only under persistent cross-
examination that the facts came to light, for the Annual
Report of the Commissioners had printed as the circular
letter of March 1 the second letter in which the word
"excessive" had been inserted.

When the dirty linen of the Commission was being
washed in public, before the Committee on the Andover
scandals in 1846, both Frankland Lewis and Chadwick
gave their version of the origin of this circular. Lewis
said that the circular was brought to the Board by
Chadwick in his absence; that the circular might well
have been kept back till his return to the office, and that

next day, when he saw it, he said to Nicholls: "I would
rather have cut off my right hand than have issued
that, if I had had an alternative." The Commissioners,
to meet his objection, agreed that future circulars should
contain the word "excessive." Chadwick denied that
he had taken deliberate advantage of Lewis's absence,
or that he had any special responsibility for the in-
clusion of this charge in the general list. The facts were
that the legal adviser had been asked to draw up such
a list, and had put the charge for tolling among them.
Chadwick had merely copied the list into his circular.
He had since urged the Commission to get a Bill passed
legalizing this and other charges. When asked whether
there was any minute recording this expression of his
views, he said he could not find one, but that he had
put the suggestion in the Fourth Report. In that Report, however, tolling the bell is not specially named.

Chadwick's defence is illuminating. His tidying mind
prompted him to put the Guardians' expenditure on a
strict and legal footing. If he had had enough imagination to realize what impression would be created by
warning the Guardians that they were not authorized by
law to pay for the rites of Christian burial, he would
never have sent out such a circular. The Guardians had
no power to alter the law; a statement of this kind from
the Commissioners was equivalent to a warning not to
break it. At a moment when a strong hand was being
laid on the indulgence and abuses that had demoralized
the Poor Law, the Commissioners went out of their way
to justify the worst that had been said of their indifference to the feelings of the poor. And Chadwick was
so insensible to the emotions that move mankind that
he never realized what a storm he was provoking.

Peel had much more understanding of the poor, and
he opposed another project, that of building workhouse
cemeteries, which had excited popular indignation. The
Rector of Petworth quoted the observation of a pauper,
that no consecration by the Bishop would change the

workhouse dung-hill into a burial-ground. An Act passed by Peel's Government, authorizing Guardians to bear the expense of burying paupers dying out of the workhouse, directed that the wishes of the dead or their friends in regard to their place of burial should be respected.

The doctrine that poverty was the consequence and the mark of bad character rather than of misfortune was not new in the England of the thirties or forties. It goes back to the harsher teaching of Puritanism; many politicians and magistrates in the eighteenth century took a merciless view of their duty to the poor. Workhouses were brutal places long before they were given the name of Bastilles. The Speenhamland system had led in some villages to practices as degrading and humiliating to the poor as any of the scandals on which Oastler and Stephens called down the wrath of God and man on Hartshead Moor. But the system of 1834, bringing many detailed improvements in the administration of the Poor Laws, gave to this doctrine a universal rigour. The workman was regarded as a person who was to be protected against the temptations of idleness by the stern choice of starvation or loss of liberty as the alternative to persistent effort. This principle was pushed to its extreme limit during the first few years of the Poor Law Commission. "By the workhouse system," Chadwick explained, "is meant having all relief through the workhouse, making this workhouse an uninviting place of wholesome restraint, preventing any of its inmates from going out or receiving visitors, without a written order to that effect from one of the Overseers; disallowing beer and tobacco, and finding them work according to their ability; thus making the parish fund the last resource of a pauper, and rendering the person who administers the relief the hardest task-master, and the worst paymaster, that the idle and dissolute can apply to." It was believed that if the workhouse were made less like a prison in any respect,

or for any class, for the unfortunate, or for the vicious,
England would slip back again into the abuses that had
scared all educated men before 1834. "What is a
pauper?" asked Cobbett, and he answered, "A very
poor man." That is what the pauper seemed to the
poor. He was a man on whom misfortune had fallen,
whether it had come as sickness or unemployment, as
the paralysis of old age, or the pinching want of the
hand-loom weaver. The logic of 1834 rested on a different conception. The pauper was as much culprit as
victim. At any rate, he was so often a culprit that it
was dangerous ever to treat him as a victim.

Another grim idea lurks in the pages of the Commissioners' Reports. Just as a slave in the ancient world
was a man who had been saved by his captor from
death by violence, so a pauper was a man who had been
saved by the overseer from death by starvation. In
both cases it was easier to think of the unfortunate as
persons with obligations to others rather than as persons with claims upon others. However harsh their
treatment, was it not better than the fate that would
have otherwise have overtaken them? Thus the workhouse assumed in all its aspects, whether as refuge or
deterrent, a penal and degrading look. Yet, of the men
and women who listened to Stephens asserting that God
had given to every man the right to live, nine out of
ten, whether they were industrious or idle, skilled or
ignorant, knew that no effort of their own could make
them secure from the danger that hung like a cloud over
the working-class world.

CHAPTER VIII

RELIGION

Anyone who studies the newspapers and periodicals that were read by the workmen at this time must be impressed by the space and energy given to the attacks on the Church. To understand the full force of this hatred we must remember that at the time of the Reform Bill the English Church was part of an aristocratic system of government, corrupted like every other part of that system by the abuses that come when the sense of possession is stronger than the sense of duty. The Church was regarded, like the pocket boroughs, as a great system of patronage and property at the disposition of the richer classes. Another cause of the Church's unpopularity was its reputation for inhumanity: the feeling that the Church sanctioned injustices that degraded the poor and outraged their self-respect. An example is provided in the agitation against flogging in the army, a barbarity that stirred working-class sentiment deeply. "What priest or swaddler [Methodist preacher] was ever known to denounce the atrocity from the pulpit," wrote the *Poor Man's Guardian* in 1833. ". . . Oh, no, the vile wretches would cant about beershops and tea-gardens and Sabbath-breaking, or anything else that afforded pleasures to the poor, but not a word would they say on behalf of the poor tortured soldier for fear of giving offence to the 'order' from which the officers are taken." Parsons who served their religion by lives of self-sacrifice and devotion made less of a mark on the imagination of the times than the parson magistrates of Peterloo, or those who threw weavers into prison on the evidence of spies.

In the early part of the nineteenth century clergymen could hold several livings together, putting curates, who were paid in some instances like the poorest labourers, in the less desirable and less healthy parishes. In 1810 there were 6,000 livings in which the incumbent was non-resident. Hay, the Vicar of Rochdale, one of the richest livings in England, was non-resident most of the time. Even as late as 1838 there were over 4,000 non-resident parsons. Chapters were as greedy and as ruthless as individuals. A Dean and Chapter would take £1,000 or £2,000 from a parish and pay somebody like Parson Andrewes to do the work for £50 a year, or even less. The Church thus combined in its ranks men with princely incomes, for which some of them rendered no service at all, and curates who were as badly off as the village labourer who was driven to live on the Speenhamland dole. With a Church so governed and inspired there was, of course, no relation between spiritual needs and the ministrations of the Church. There was not a single bishop in Lancashire or the West Riding until 1836. Churches were, like Members of Parliament, most numerous where least needed.

Soon after the passing of the Reform Bill these sensational abuses were removed, partly by the influence of reformers within the Church, partly by legislation initiated by Peel and carried on by Russell. An organ for internal reform was set up in the Ecclesiastical Commission; scandals disappeared; attempts were made to supply the neglected districts by new bishoprics at Manchester and Ripon; the glaring inequality between the incomes of different sees was removed; members of Chapters were forbidden to hold more than one benefice or to belong to more than one Chapter, and it was made illegal to hold two benefices if they were more than a mile apart, or if the additional stipend exceeded £1,000.

With these reforms disappeared the resounding scandals that had filled so many sparkling pages in the Radical pamphlets of the time. Cobbett's *Legacy to Parsons* was now a book for the library shelf rather than

the political platform; a stern hand had been laid on
the corruption which had displayed so splendid a target
for his incomparable invective. This was a great achievement, but it would be false to say of it that it had solved
the urgent problem that faced the Church. It was one
thing to put an end to sinecures and abuses and to give
a serious and responsible character to the office of its
parsons, hitherto regarded and held with such levity;
it was another to satisfy the imagination of the great
population on whose daily life of bleak and monotonous
toil those civilizing influences to which mankind has
looked for comfort, ever since the first city found shelter
behind its circling walls, shed so pale and doubtful a
light. How far could the Church succeed in helping men
and women to turn away from the hard face of a
struggle, in which wealth brought fame, and poverty
contempt, to this mysterious atmosphere, where the soul
of Dives was no more esteemed than the soul of Laza-
rus? The importance of religion, like the importance of
culture or the importance of beauty, in the social setting examined in these pages depended on its power to
create a world of its own, with standards, duties, and
satisfactions other than those set and sought in the race
for wealth.

There is an important aspect of early Christianity
which should be remembered in considering this question. Historians have shown how widespread was the
discontent of the submerged world before the advent of
Christianity; how ardently men were dreaming of
equality and fellowship. The most striking quality in the
early Church, the Church of the first three centuries,
from which Augustine drew his picture of the City of
God, is described in Toynbee's phrase, "a rival civilization of the proletariat." In a dialogue by a writer of the
second century A.D. (Minucius Felix), the pagan is made
to reproach Christianity with collecting the dregs of the
people, and the Christian replies that this is not a reproach but a glory. Early Christian churches gave effect

to revolutionary ideas in their daily life and practice, abolishing, not only in the dreams of philosophers, but before the eyes of men, the distinctions between rich and poor, bond and free, bringing, as Tarn puts it, to those who laboured and were heavy laden a different hope. In the age of which we write there was ample room for this kind of Christianity, as we can see from the success of the Chartist Churches, where the spirit and teaching of early Christianity attracted large numbers of men and women who found Church and Chapel alike cold and unsympathetic. The earliest of these Churches was started in Scotland, but they soon spread to England. The Midland Mining Commission (1843) described their widespread influence in Birmingham and the mining districts, where the preacher O'Neill, a prominent Chartist, seems to have become as great a power among the miners as Wesley himself had been a century earlier in Cornwall and Somerset. But, however great the need, the Established Church and the Methodists alike were, with some striking exceptions, hampered by their difficulties from playing this part in the life of the new proletariat.

The difficulties of the Church were not new; they were almost as old as Christianity. Dr. Gore has described in his vivid sketch, "Christ and Society," the changes that came over Christianity with the "transition from a Church sometimes grudgingly tolerated, and sometimes fiercely persecuted, to a Church seated in the high places of government and power." The Church never afterwards found it easy to become what it had tried to be in early days, "a spiritual aristocracy which could draw and convert the world by the spectacle of a life so different from its own."

The English Church, though freed from its worst abuses, still stood for resignation to the established order and consideration for the rich. A fundamental difficulty was described by Bishop Blomfield in his evidence before the Committee on the Observance of the Sabbath,

in 1832: "It is the object of the Commissioners for
building new churches, as far as they can, to inter-
mingle the seats of the rich and the poor, so as to afford
the latter nearly the same facilities for hearing which the
former enjoy. We have found considerable difficulty in
realizing our own wishes in that respect, on account of
the objections which were made by the richer classes to
too great an intermixture of the poor among them,
objections which it was absolutely necessary to attend
to because the whole income of the Minister depends on
the pew rents accruing exclusively from the richer
classes." This custom of charging rents for pews, a custom common not only in newly founded mission churches
but in existing parish churches, was greatly resented by
the working classes, as was shown by the action of the
Chartists who protested against the practice, which they
considered a violation of the right of the people to their
parish churches. Large numbers used to assemble before
the hours of service, march to church, and occupy the
reserved pews. This was done in all the chief towns in
1839; in Manchester, Bradford, Newcastle, Bristol, Norwich, Bolton, Blackburn, Stockport, and other places.
Disraeli said in *Sybil* that this plan very much affected
"the imagination of the multitude." Sometimes the
Chartists gave notice to the parson, and even suggested
a text. Dr. Whittaker, of Blackburn, having been invited to preach on the text, "Go to now, ye rich, weep
and howl for your miseries that are coming upon you,"
explained that these words had no application to England "governed by equal laws." At Manchester the
preacher substituted his own text: " My house is a house
of prayer, but you have made it a den of thieves." At
Bury "the worthy Rector being fully prepared for their
visit, gave them a lecture on keeping the peace and
obeying the law, which from its length, as well as from
its force, many of them would not exactly relish." In a
few instances there was disorder. In most of the churches
the Chartists had to listen to critical sermons, but on

one occasion they were specially invited to attend the
Roman Catholic Church at Norwich, where the
preacher, taking as his text, "Let him that hath two
coats impart to him that hath none," preached an inflammatory sermon on the Reformation, and the wrongs
done by Protestants to the poor.

But if the Church, in spite of its reforms and new
activity, still had these difficulties, what about the
Methodists, who, unlike the Church, were not identi-
fied with the governing classes? To answer this we must
look back at the history of Methodism. About the character of the Methodist revival, the most important event
in eighteenth-century England, there is general agreement. It was one of the periodical outbursts of
vitality that have marked the history of Christianity;
for its predecessors we must turn to the great movements associated with such names as those of St.
Benedict, St. Francis, John Wycliffe, and John Huss.
Its founder created a body of preachers who resembled
the early disciples of St. Francis, alike in their relation
to the religion in power, and in their view of their own
mission. Their business was not to teach a new theology,
but to bring ardour and purpose into a Church whose
teaching had become formal and cold, and whose life
and conduct reflected and respected too faithfully the
spirit and outlook of the world. They were not rebels
against the authority of this indolent and comfortable
institution; they were rebels against the easy-going
pagan life of the time, with its neglect of the passionate
gospel which the Christian Church came to life to preach.
The Church had become more like a school of social
manners than a witness to a militant faith; there was no
note of indignation or rapture in its pulpits. The Methodists desired to supply the fervour that was lacking.
They were not Nonconformists but revivalists, and they
succeeded in reviving both the Established and the Nonconformist Churches. The relation in which they stood
to the Church was well illustrated by the rules that

Wesley laid down forbidding preachers to hold services in Church hours unless the incumbent was a "notoriously wicked man" or unless he preached Arian or "equally pernicious doctrine."

These early preachers resembled the Franciscans in another respect. They practised an austere simplicity of life; they were to make themselves conspicuous amid the levity of the age by their earnest and solemn behaviour. A strict discipline was required of them. They were not to use tobacco for "smoking, chewing, or snuff," except on doctor's orders; they were to fast; they were to avoid spirituous liquors; they were 'to converse sparingly and cautiously with women, particularly with young women"; preachers desiring to marry were to consult their brethren, and any member who married an unbeliever was to be expelled. They were bidden expressly not to affect the gentleman, but to remember that a preacher of the Gospel is the servant of all.

Religion has been defined by Professor Whitehead as "what a man does with his solitariness," and in this sense it may be as self-regarding as any other activity. It may take a man no farther than his own shadow. For it may take him from his material cares and ambitions to plunge him in meditations in which his own life in a different aspect is still the centre. "Methodism with its eye forever turned on its own navel; asking itself with torturing anxiety of Hope and Fear, 'Am I right? am I wrong? Shall I be saved? shall I not be damned?' —what is this," asked Carlyle, "at bottom, but a new phasis of *Egoism*, stretched out into the Infinite? not always the heavenlier for its infinitude!" Carlyle's description was true of one kind of Methodist. But, of course, a man may do with his solitariness something nobler than this. The chapels, if they found a home for men and women tormented by such anxieties, found a home also for men and women in whose passionate desire for communion with God "the unseen took shape to common eye." In this way religion made numbers

of men and women happier, more unselfish, more ready
to pity the sorrows of their fellow men, more ready to
undertake burdens for their relief. The Methodist movement did for eighteenth-century England what Christianity did for the ancient world, giving to men of conscience and compassion a cause for which to live, and
blending the idea of the brotherhood of man with the
most sublime of the mysteries of religion.

There is, however, a sense in which religion is not
what a man does with his solitariness, but what a man
does with his gregariousness. Religion gave its colour to
the collective imagination of the primitive village watching anxiously the seasons of sowing and harvest. Sometimes in the history of the world it has almost filled
the content of that imagination. You could not say of
Churchmen or Methodists or Baptists that they were
merely so many men and women worshipping in their
own way without any common life or any common influence. "Christianity is first of all a way of life in
fellowship." Fellowship takes a man out of his solitariness. These religious bodies were not only bodies of men
holding certain beliefs and practising religious observ-
ances; they were bodies of people with a discipline
affecting social conduct.

A moral revolt is always apt to answer extravagance
by extravagance. The Methodist revolt was no exception. It was a revolt against dissolute manners, and it
demanded ascetic manners. Wesley was proud, it will
be remembered, that the Methodists abstained from
"reading plays, romances, or books of humour, from
singing innocent songs, or talking in a gay, diverting
manner." He said that to educate a man you must
break his will, and when he drew the rules for his
school at Kingswood he said that he allowed no time for
play, because he who plays as a boy will play when he
is a man. If a man puts play outside his life, he sur-
renders tastes and pleasures that are an essential part
of human history: the source of much of the beauty, the

grace, the power, and the virtue, that distinguish higher from lower forms of character and intelligence. A man or a society may make that sacrifice for a particular object. And a man who has renounced something, taking stern vows upon himself, at the bidding of conscience, is richer as well as poorer. For an ascetic life touches the imagination of the man who chooses it, since deliberate sacrifice is an act of resolution, bringing the satisfaction that comes from living your life at a bracing pitch. But to serve this purpose, an ascetic life must be the choice of the man who leads it. When an ascetic life is thrust on others, it deprives them of opportunities for satisfying their imagination in which mankind has found light and inspiration, and puts nothing in their place.

The influence of this spirit was spread over the life of the time, and had a profound effect, through the Evangelical movement, on the Church. The decline of the theatre was largely due to it. The last half of the eighteenth century has been described by Lecky as the golden age of the English drama: "It saw Garrick, Macklin, and Barry in their prime; it witnessed the splendid rise of John Kemble and Mrs. Siddons, as well as the lighter graces of Miss Farren, Mrs. Jordan, and Mrs. Abington, and at a time when the great Shakespearean revival was its height it also produced the plays of Goldsmith, Sheridan, Foote, and Home. There was an incontestable improvement in the moral tendency, and still more in the refinement of the theatre, and it was noticed that a coarseness which excited no reprobation under George I was no longer tolerated on the stage. The revolt of popular feeling against the legislative discouragement of the theatre had now become very marked." This revolt showed itself in the evasion of the Act of 1737, which had confined the legitimate drama to the Haymarket, Covent Garden, and Drury Lane, and also in the money spent by the large towns to obtain a special Act of Parliament to enable them to set up a theatre. In this way theatres were provided between 1767 and 1775 in Edinburgh, Bath, Bristol, York, Hull, Liverpool, Manchester, and Chester. In 1778 a concession was made, and magistrates were allowed to grant licences for special performances for 60 days. Tate Wilkinson, an actor, took companies to the North of England, where good plays were given, either in Theatres Royal set up by special Act of Parliament, or in theatres licensed on this plan. Mrs. Siddons, Mrs. Jordan, and other good actors visited the provinces every year.

If anybody had been told in 1780 that in the next half-century the English people would grow much richer; that the picture given in his book by Tate Wilkinson, of the country gentlemen round Wakefield who supported his theatre there, would seem modest in comparison with the wealth that would spring up round all the new towns; that every industrial town would have a large, comfortable class with leisure; that this accession of wealth would be accompanied by a burst of literary power; he might well have supposed that the theatre would play a great part in the life of this time, and help to guide and inspire the imagination of the great population whose fortunes have been followed in these pages. What would have seemed more natural than that writers who were masters of another literary form, like Scott and Dickens, would turn to the drama, as Fielding and Goldsmith had turned to it in the eighteenth century, and as Galsworthy and Bennett were to turn to it in the twentieth; that Dickens, who was to do more to draw English people together than any other influence in the time, would write comedies, as he wrote novels, that rich and poor alike could enjoy? What would have been the surprise of such a person to be told that the theatre would rapidly decline, that in 1853 there would be one theatre in Manchester and no theatre at all in Salford, and that in 1873 Kingsley would be able to write: "Few highly educated men now think it worth while to go to

see any play, and that exactly for the same reasons as
the Puritans put forward; and still fewer highly educated
men think it worth while to write plays; finding that
since the grosser excitements of the imagination have
become forbidden themes, there is really very little to
write about."

There were, of course, more causes than one for this
remarkable decline. The law was still adverse in certain
ways. Down to 1834 dramatic authors had no protection, and provincial theatres could act a piece that had
been given in London, without paying the author anything. It was not until 1843 that magistrates were
allowed to license theatres. More general reasons are to
be found in the rise of the cheap print and rival attractions. But undoubtedly one cause was the influence of
the Methodists. That influence was exerted with some
success even in the early days of Methodism. In 1764
John Wesley wrote to the Mayor and Corporation of
Bristol protesting against the proposal to build a theatre,
not merely because "most of the present stage enter-
tainments sap the foundation of all religion," but also
because a theatre would be "peculiarly hurtful to a
trading city, giving a wrong turn to youth especially,
gay, trifling, and directly opposite to the spirit of industry and close application to business." He added
that the Corporation of Nottingham had been led by
these considerations to forbid the building of a new
theatre. Wesley was using here an argument that served
for men who were not Methodists. Thus, Archbishop
Cornwallis—not much of a Methodist in his own habits,
for his Sunday parties at Lambeth drew down a rebuke
from George III—opposed the Manchester Playhouse
Bill in 1775 on the ground that theatres encouraged
idleness in industrial towns. Tate Wilkinson had to encounter strong opposition in the provinces, and he
described the outbursts of a clergyman of the Low
Church at Hull, who declared that "everyone who entered a playhouse was, with the players, equally certain

of eternal damnation." As Methodism spread among the
employing class, this influence spread in the industrial
towns. Dickens deplored the effect in discouraging the
theatre and encouraging less desirable substitutes. Three
months before his death he wrote that "the narrow-
minded fanatics who decry the theatre and defame its
artists are absolutely the advocates of depraved and
barbarous amusements. For wherever a good drama and
well-regulated theatre decline, some distorted form of
theatrical entertainment will inevitably arise in their
place." He pointed out that this moral had been urged
in *Hard Times*.

The Methodists did with the English Sunday what they
did with the English theatre. For the mass of the working classes there was only one day on which they were
free from the discipline of mill and workshop. On that
day they were refused recreation for mind or body,
music or games, beauty of art or nature. They sought
diversions where they could find them. The Yorkshire
and Lancashire papers are full of complaints that the
youth of the large towns spent Sunday gambling in the
streets, or in drunkenness and brutal sports, and that
the behaviour of the populace was distressing and in-
convenient to respectable people. An engineer who had
been abroad described the difference in this respect between English and Continental life. He told the Factory
Commission that at Mülhausen, where most of the
people were Protestant, the workmen went to church
in the morning and spent the rest of the day in the
country playing games, whereas in England "a man can
do nothing but go to a public house on Sunday, and
when there you can do nothing but drink." Chadwick,
who cited the engineer's evidence, suggested to the Committee on Drunkenness that public gardens should be
provided with free admission after morning service on
Sundays. Unhappily Sabbatarian prejudice was too
strong, and the English people were left to gloom and
drink.

The fate of the Botanical Gardens at Leeds is a good illustration of this Puritan feeling. The Gardens did not pay, and when the shareholders decided to give them up, it was proposed that the Town Council should acquire them. The *Leeds Intelligencer* gave strong support to this proposal, suggesting that they should be thrown open on Sundays, as that was the only day when the working classes could enjoy them. This was too bold a plan for respectable Leeds, whose scruples were well represented in a leading article that was published a few months later in the *Leeds Mercury* on the subject of Sabbath observance. "It would be a wretched exchange to draw the poor of England out of their Churches, Chapels, Sunday-schools and quiet homes into public exhibitions and places of amusement on the Lord's Day." The "quiet homes" in which the poor of Leeds were invited to spend their happy Sundays included a good many houses of the kind described by Mr. Robert Baker in his Sanitary Report, where fourteen people lay ill of typhus, without a single bed in the place.

Leeds was not peculiar in this respect. At Liverpool we read, "on Sundays . . . all the public walks, cemeteries, and zoological and botanical gardens, where the people might amuse themselves innocently, are closed." "Have the public a right of going to those gardens on any day?"—"Not the public generally; but the cemeteries are opened to the public every day of week except Sunday." Manchester was under the same cloud. *The North of England Magazine* published a series of sketches describing the life of that city in 1842, and the shutting of the Zoological Gardens on Sundays was cited as one of the worst injustices inflicted on the mass of the population. The writer quoted a French observer Bruet, who remarked: "The observance of the Sunday in England is rigorously enforced by church and state. There is only one exception: the dram shops. All shops must be closed, all places of innocent amusement or instruction, such as Botannical

The Methodists made one notable contribution. By a happy fortune the two Wesleys were poets and musicians, and singing became an important feature of Methodist services. Wesley published a book of hymns and tunes "designed chiefly for the use of the people called Methodist," and in his *Journal* he described from time to time the pleasure with which he had noticed the progress of music. In 1787 he founded a Sunday School at Bolton, with eight hundred children, of whom a hundred were taught singing. He was disturbed by a tendency in some places to introduce more formal music, and he drew up rules for the guidance of chapels. Anthems were not to be sung; great care was to be taken in training; and the whole congregation was to be exhorted to sing, "not one in ten only." Coleridge said that the hearty congregational singing of English hymns kept the Methodists together, and Horace Mann, when commenting on the figures of the Religious Census, said that the Methodists had discovered a form of service specially suitable for poor people.

With this exception, music played little part in the religious life of the time. Wesley, fearing quarrels over the introduction of organs, said that no organ was to be placed in a chapel until it was proposed in Conference. One of the fiercest controversies in the Methodist world arose over a conflict at Brunswick Street Chapel, Leeds, in 1828, on this question. A later writer remarked that at this time poor men and women in the Yorkshire towns used to save up their pennies for an oratorio, and yet religious bodies were very slow to satisfy this desire in public worship. Bishop Blomfield deprecated the introduction of cathedral services, the use of surplices, and processions, and when a clergyman wrote describing the ordinary church services as "blank, dismal, oppressive, and dreary," he replied, "If the minister *reads* with devotion and sincerity (not *intones*); if the congregation join in the responses and psalmody; and if sound doctrine and practical exhortations be earnestly and affectionately delivered by the preacher, such epithets as you have used are grievously mis-applied." Raumer, a German visitor, thought the want of musical education for the people was a result of the way in which Sunday was observed.

Religion was thus making little use of the arts. Music made its way slowly and with difficulty; there were few imposing ceremonies in church; no rich and noble pageants in the streets, to bring history into the life of Hunslet or Ancoats. The new churches, in which the Gothic revival prevailed, were too often, in spite of the Tractarian opposition to pew rents, like the adver-tisement quoted with scorn by the High Church periodi-cal, the *British Critic*. "Plan and elevation for a Gothic church upon a large scale, to seat upwards of 1,500 persons. . . . The handsome vestibule entrance with an enriched groined ceiling, and the noble staircase on each side, which lead to the gallery, give to the design a grand and noble effect, suitable to the character of a wealthy and extensive parish. Here are also a numb of free seats." It is possible that some satisfaction was found for the starved dramatic sense of the age in the rhetoric, so common then in church and chapel, which painted the torments of everlasting fire. It is significant that the biographer of the famous Methodist preacher, William Dawson, speaking of his power as a pulpit orator, chose his handling of this topic as the best example of his gifts. Dawson told his terrified hearers that a man's torments in hell would be all the fiercer because his parents had prayed for him. This stern and forbidding Sunday, with its sanctions of childish terror, its "codes of fearful fantasy," was the gift of religion to a people needing above all things some space in its life in which it could lose itself in noble wonder, in the enjoyment of form or sound, in submission to ideas that could stir the spirit of fellowship and communion. "The lower classes," said Raumer, "who often have to toil wearily through every other day, find Sunday, as it is constantly described, the weariest of all. Often after serving an austere master, they are made to find in the Father of Love, an austerer still.''

The Church had yet a further difficulty, at this time, due to the very conditions in which it had awakened. Two movements had brought power and purpose into its life: the Evangelical movement had brought earnestness and devotion, the Tractarian movement had brought a wider and deeper sense of the place of religion in history and civilization. The great change in the character and spirit of the clergy, which is apparent if we contrast 1850 with 1800, is the result largely of these two movements. But unfortunately the movements were rivals, and bitter rivals, and at this time they were chiefly occupied with their controversies. The Church which had to overtake the neglect of half a century was thus disabled and distracted by its internal conflicts. Dr. Gore has remarked that after the third century the emphasis in the history of the Christian Church passed from right living to right thinking, from conduct to orthodoxy. Something like this happened in early Victorian England. The Church was full of vitality and movement, rich in thinkers, teachers, men of saintly life and serious scholarship. Newman, Pusey, Maurice, Robertson, and Whately were all helping to form the English mind of the next generation, but in the days when Chartism was spreading over the towns, this intellectual vigour found its expression in the bitter strife of Evangelical and Tractarian. ''The conviction has been brought home to some of us with terrible force,'' wrote F. D. Maurice, ''that while religious men are disputing . . . the great body of Englishmen is becoming bitterly indifferent to us all and smiles grimly and contemptuously at our controversies.'' While the party men led by ''theological champions armed at all points'' were filling the Church with the sound of conflict, the mass of the poor in most of the great towns remained outside it.

Methodism, like the Church, had its difficulties, the difficulties that are brought by success. In the eighteenth century Methodism was in its spirit more like the early Church than the Church as it became under Constantine's ægis. It won its greatest triumphs among the poor. Wesley and his disciples converted whole districts, like the mining parts of Cornwall, from a life of dissipation and plunder to devout and orderly habits. All over England and Wales great numbers of ignorant men and women were brought for the first time under religion's spell.

In some parts of England and Wales Methodism was still a Revivalist movement in the forties. Thus the Commission on the Employment of Children in 1843 gave a glowing account of the work done by the Methodists in districts like the Forest of Dean and North Wales, closely resembling the descriptions of Wesley's work in Cornwall. The colliers had been the terror of the surrounding country "for gross ignorance, rudeness, and irreligion, almost without parallel in any Christian community." Churches there were none except on the extreme outskirts; the great area of the Forest being extra-parochial, though very populous, and schools were almost unknown. In this district a striking change had been produced by the work of the Dissenters. "The success of their zeal is everywhere exhibited in the immense number of chapels which have been built within the last thirty years. The money to build them has been drawn from the pockets of the farmers, small tradesmen, and the working orders, by means of penny subscriptions in the chapels, to which even the boys who are earning wages contribute." So in North Wales: "What the established Church has not yet been able to supply, the Dissenters have; chapels have everywhere been built by them, and their efforts, always unsupported and often scoffed at by the clergy, gentry, and influential proprietors, have been attended with signal success."

In many industrial districts, on the other hand, Methodism was rather one of the settled religions than a new and passionate gospel. It was no longer despised or persecuted, but it was no longer a religion of the proletariat. Horace Mann, who drew up the Report on the Religious Census of 1851, said that most of the new chapels had been built for the middle classes, and that as the towns separated into respectable and proletarian districts, the poor were worse off in this respect as in others. The Irish immigrants probably suffered less, for they had their Catholic chapels and priests in their midst, and it is significant that in the cholera epidemics the deaths of Catholic priests are often noted in the papers. Faucher said that he did not see the working classes in the chapels of Manchester and Leeds. The people walking along the streets belonged exclusively to the middle classes. The operatives loitered at their doors or lounged at street corners until the hour of service was over and the public houses open. Methodism, in losing its first missionary character, had fallen to some extent under the shadow of respectability. In early days the weavers used to attend chapel with their aprons rolled round their waists, and some of them had thought that to drop their aprons would mean that they had conformed to the world. These democratic habits had disappeared. In 1842 the Annual Report of the Wesleyan Methodist Conference regretted that in times of distress the poor neglected chapel "because a want of suitable clothing leaves a meanness in their appearance which is chiefly conspicuous for its being contrasted with that of the more favoured of their brethren." A witness before the Health of Towns Commission drew the line between those who could dress for chapel and those who could not. "The general practice is, on the Sunday evening, for those who are not able to make a decent appearance at a place of worship to congregate together, pay their halfpenny or penny, and send for a newspaper from a public-house."

The distinction between the respectable and the common people was emphasized in chapel as in church, by the distinction between pews and free seats. The distinction had brought with it all the dangers that Wesley dreaded, for Wesley had stood out against the system of pew rents. In Wesley's London headquarters, the Foundry, "all benches were alike. No difference was made here between the rich and the poor; no one was allowed to call any seat his own, first-comers sat down first." In December 1787 Wesley had a difference with his Committee on this point, and his language shows what a serious view he took of the threatened change. "The Committee proposed to me . . . that everyone who took a pew should have it as his own. Thus overturning, at one blow, the discipline which I had been establishing for fifty years." Three days later he reports the satisfactory result of the discussion. "We had another meeting of the Committee, who after a calm and loving consultation, judged it best that none should claim any pew of his own, either in the new chapel or in West Street." But Wesley's principle did not long survive him.

"Our chapels," wrote a leading Wesleyan minister in the *Watchman* in 1849, "have been fitted up too much as private dwellings than as places of public worship; and the free sittings, if sufficient, not made readily perceivable nor easily accessible. I could name chapels with expensive architectural frontispieces of stone and with interior ornaments of 'dead white and gold' where the poor's seats are like sheep-pens, in the four corners of the building and behind the pulpit; and where, even then, the seats adjoining are screened off most carefully by high rods and curtains. I am no believer in the doctrine of 'equality' as it is now expounded by many— I regard it as foolish and contrary to the order of God. . . . But admitting all this, it is not only unbecoming but detrimental to Methodism (and it would be so to any church) thus to appear to neglect the poor."

Early in his career Wesley had been concerned for the future of Methodism. "I do not see," he wrote in 1787, "how it is possible in the nature of things for any revival of religion to continue long. For religion must necessarily produce both Industry and Frugality and these cannot but produce Riches. But as Riches increase so will Pride, Anger, and Love of the World in all its branches." Nobody could deny that so far as the influence of Methodism in the great towns was concerned, Wesley's fears had come true. Halévy, in his brilliant study, described Puritan Nonconformity as "a stage in the history of the English family. The unskilled labourer becomes in turn a skilled workman, an artisan, the head of a small business, a business·man possessed of a modest capital, and as he rises out of the barbarism in which the working class was plunged, he becomes a Nonconformist." Methodists made industrious and successful workmen, tradesmen, managers, and employers. It was natural for men in this atmosphere to think that if a man was poor it was the consequence of his own wickedness. A leading Nonconformist, giving evidence on Church rates, remarked: "Religion always tends to give a man the power to pay for his religion and the will." One of Galsworthy's characters says much the same in the *Skin Game*: "God helps those who help themselves, that is at the bottom of all religion." As Methodism became a settled system it tended to take rather than give a standard. The spirit of the age put its bias and character on Methodism as on everything else. The rich man of the Bible, who found it so difficult to enter the Kingdom of Heaven, had been succeeded by the rich man of the Puritan revival who stepped into wealth and Paradise from the same ladder. For the rich man was no longer the idle man, who enjoyed himself while others toiled; he was the industrious man who made others richer by his industry. Thus success and failure, achievement and defeat, had come to look very much the same inside and outside the chapel. If some-

body had said to a prosperous Methodist of Manchester
or Leeds, as the pagan of the second century had said
to the Christian, that his religion collected the dregs of
the people, the Methodist would have considered it not
a glory but a reproach.

CHAPTER IX

EDUCATION

In 1834 the passion for social improvement and for accurate information induced a body of gentlemen in Manchester, who had formed a Statistical Society, to start an inquiry into the state of education in that town. The inquiry spread to neighbouring towns, to Salford, Liverpool, Bury, Bolton, Ashton, Dukinfield, Stalybridge, and even to York. Later, Birmingham and Bristol were also investigated in the same way. The results were digested and published in different reports, mostly between 1834 and 1837, and, from the remarks of the investigators, even more than from the numerous statistical tables, it is possible to form some estimate of the opportunities for schooling at that time. There was no compulsory attendance except for children working in factories, and there the schooling existed chiefly on paper.

Let us suppose that the parents of a small intelligent boy in Manchester, of what we should now call school age, were anxious that he should learn his letters and whatever else he could pick up. In 84 out of the 86 Sunday-schools in Manchester, he would be taught to read after a fashion, and in 10 of those schools he might learn writing too, but the process would be long and tedious, and we will suppose that his parents wished for instruction on week days. He would first be sent to one of the many Dame Schools scattered about the town (there were 230 of them in Manchester), where reading, and, for girls, sewing, were taught. If he were lucky he would live close to one of the old-fashioned type, where a tidy old lady would teach habits of neatness, even though her literary standards were not high. If he were very fortunate he would find himself at the school "kept by a blind man who hears his scholars their lessons and explains them with great simplicity." The blind teacher was liable to be interrupted by being called to turn his wife's mangle, but probably the lessons were none the worse for that. If he were less fortunate he would find that the Dame School was a dirty, close room, where children were sent not so much to learn as "to be taken care of and to be out of the way at home,"—"If I can keep a bit of quietness," said one of the Dames, "it is as much as I can do and as much as I am paid for"— where books to read and fresh air to breathe were equally scarce, where discipline depended on the rod, where the only saving grace was a certain slackness so that in hot weather, for instance, the children could stretch out their limbs (provided there were room) on forms or floor, and sleep away the weary afternoon. As a Bury mistress remarked with truth, by way of apology, "they were better so than awake." For the privilege of sending a child to one of these Dame Schools parents paid as a rule 4d. a week, some more, some less. The average income of the Manchester Dames was calculated to be £17 16s. or 6s. 10d. a week, in Bury it was put at £19 a year. It was supplemented by earnings from other sources such as shopkeeping, sewing, or washing. Teaching might be combined with keeping a cake shop, for which the pupils provided a clientele, or with selling milk, in which case the scholars could amuse themselves with dabbling in the cans. Occasionally the poor rates provided the necessary supplement, but this was rare.

In his next stage the boy would go to what the Statistical Society called a "Common Day School," that is a school kept by a master or mistress who made his or her living by it. This was the type of school at which the majority of boys and girls in Manchester obtained their education, such as it was. The charge was higher than at the Dame Schools, from 6d. to 9d. a week, and the average master made 16s. or 17s. a week, the capable master a good deal more. Too often the teacher's qualification for his job was that noted in the case of the old men who kept Dame Schools: "unfitness for every other." These masters and mistresses, however, had a better opinion of themselves than that held by their investigators. "Some intelligent masters," it was said, ". . . conceive there is something in the occupation which begets self-sufficiency." Whatever the truth of this, these Common Day School masters were "strongly impressed with the superiority of their own plans to those of any other school, and very little inclined to listen to any suggestions respecting improvements in the system of education that had been made in other places." These schools professed to teach reading, writing, and arithmetic. Penmanship was considered essential, and specimens of fine writing were exhibited to attract parents. In some of the better ones a little grammar and geography were thrown in for an extra penny or so a week. Occasionally they soared higher. In one school the master dilated on the various sciences he could teach: Hydraulics, Hydrostatics, Geography, Geology, Etymology, Entomology. The visitor remarked: "This is *multum in parvo* indeed." To which the master immediately replied: "Yes, I teach that: you may put that down too."

The premises of these schools were not much better than those of the Dame Schools. Perhaps the worst example was a school in Liverpool, where a garret, measuring 10 feet by 9 feet, contained one master, one cock, two hens, three black terriers, and forty children. Bad air, dirty rooms, incompetent teachers, disorderly ways ("tiresome task this teaching," remarked one master, "there is no managing them"), absence of books or other apparatus, were characteristics of these schools. A floating population of boys and girls resorted to them; in most boys' schools there were some girls, and in most girls' schools some boys, and the children learnt or failed to learn the elements of the three R's, to the constant accompaniment of the birch. On the other hand, the masters and mistresses were occasionally persons of ability, and even when ability was absent there was also an absence of the monotony and routine which improved methods often brought with them. School life must have had attractions and surprises under the master who was met by the investigator "issuing from his school at the head of all his scholars, to see a fight in the neighbourhood; and instead of stopping to reply to any educational queries, only uttered a breathless invitation to come along and see the sport." These schools were severely blamed for their neglect of any systematic religious and moral instruction, but a good many children surfeited with this teaching in National or Lancasterian schools might have done better in the care of the master who, when asked his method of religious teaching, answered "I hear them their catechism once a week," and to the question how he taught morals, replied, "I tell them to be good lads, you know, and mind what I say to them, and so on." Perhaps they might have done no worse under the gentleman who, when asked if he taught morals, observed: "That question does not belong to my school, it belongs to the girls' schools." One of these masters, held up to ridicule in the Manchester Report, seems to have been before his time. He stated that "he had adopted a system which he thought would at once supply the great desiderata in education. 'It is simply,' he said, 'in watching the dispositions of the children and putting them especially to that particular thing which they take to.' In illustration of this system, he called up a boy of about ten years of age, who had *taken to* Hebrew, and was just beginning to learn it; the master acknowledging that he himself was learning too, in order to teach his pupil. On being asked whether he did not now and then find a few who did not take to anything, he acknowledged that it was so, and this, he said, was the only weak point in his system, as he feared that he should not be able to make much of those children.

It might have happened that the boy whose experi-

ences we are attempting to imagine, instead of going
one of the ramshackle, self-supporting schools, went
instead to a school dependent on public subscription and
conducted on the lines of one of the two societies for
educating the poor, whose methods and rivalries fill so
much of the educational literature of the time. In the
Manchester Lancasterian School, connected with the
British and Foreign School Society, he would have
found over a thousand close-packed children, sitting on
benches, all being taught together in one room, with
only two masters and one mistress in charge. At first the
noise would have been deafening, the crowd bewildering,
but soon he would have noticed that there was order and
system in the apparent chaos, that the multitude obeyed
certain words and commands such as "sling hats,"
"clean slates," and acted as one child, that each nine
or ten boys were in charge of another boy called a
monitor, who taught them the lesson that he had lately
learned himself, either summoning them to stand round
him in one of the semicircles marked in the passage at
the end of the forms and teaching them to read from a
board with the lesson printed large upon it, or else
standing at the end of the form on which they were
sitting and dictating to them words of the number of
syllables suitable to their particular class. Dictation for
the whole school was a triumph of organization. On the
platform at one end sat the master, and at a signal from
him, or from the "monitor-general," a sort of sergeant-
major among children, the monitor of the highest class
would lead off with his four-syllabled word, followed in
turn by each monitor in the hierarchy down to the
bottom. When the process had been repeated for six
words, each monitor examined the slates of his charges
and signalled to the master by means of a "telegraph"
or signboard fixed at the end of the form; as soon as
corrections were made, and all the telegraphs turned the
right way, the master gave the signal again and another
six words were dictated.

If the boy were specially bright he might find himself, even at the early age of seven, chosen by the master to be trained as a monitor. The master would teach him a lesson and he would repeat it like a little gramophone to his small group. His authority over his group or "draft" would not extend to chastisement, but he was expected to become a rather stern disciplinarian. If he perceived "a pupil untidy, talking, or idle," it was "his duty to put a disgrace or accusation-mark about his neck, having first warned him." He was to take away the disgrace-mark as soon as the pupil showed that he was corrected of his fault, or as soon as he perceived "that another pupil had committed a similar offence." "Incorrigible pupils" he would send up to the master's platform. Even these boys were not whipped, for in marked contrast to the Common Day Schools, the Lancasterian and National Schools trusted to a system of rewards and of confinement for their discipline. Dirty boys were "sentenced to have their faces and hands washed before the whole school and to be confined for half an hour"; talkers, players, and idlers were also given half an hour's confinement, but by an ingenious arrangement of barter each half-hour's confinement could be paid for by a "merit ticket." But those culprits whose supply of tickets failed were "taken to the bottom of the school by the monitor of bad boys," and there made to do dictation of an appropriate kind for the allotted period. Good boys and monitors could exchange their merit tickets, each of which was worth half a farthing, for books or clothing at the end of the month.

School began and ended with the reading by the master of a chapter of the Bible; the Bible was the only reading-book, and on the Bible all lessons were based. In some schools there were libraries from which the more promising pupils might borrow books to read out of school hours, but these books generally had "a bearing towards the works of God or the word of God." By 1831, in order to counteract the deadly effects of mechanical instruction which were very obvious, attempts were made to teach the children the meaning of the words or sentences that they read or spelt or wrote, by a system of interrogation that had been hitherto confined to the highest class. Thus if the reading lesson had consisted of the first verse of Genesis, the following interrogation would take place:

"*Monitor*. Who created the heavens and the earth?
  Pupil. God.
  Monitor. When did God create the heavens and the earth?
  Pupil. In the beginning.
  Monitor. What did God do in the beginning?
  Pupil. He created the heavens and the earth," etc., etc.

If the boy remained long enough at school he would learn reading, writing, and the first four rules of arithmetic; if he stayed longer he would be instructed in "geography both ancient and modern." This, as we shall see, contained also scraps of historical information. We will take a sample lesson, which was the ideal for the most forward children. Tyre was the subject. The monitor had loaded his own mind with various particulars about Tyre, acquired either from the master or from books studied in the school library. He would then, supposing there was a map, put it up, point out the position of Tyre, and proceed to relate his various items of information. After this he would question them on what he had told them, as follows:

"*Monitor*. Where is it?"
  Pupil. On an Island.
  Monitor. Describe the situation of the Island?
  Pupil. It is at the eastern extremity of the Levant, opposite the northern part of the Holy Land, from which it is separated by a narrow strait.

Monitor. What occasioned its erection on an Island?

Pupil. Its being attacked by Nebuchadnezzar.

Monitor. In what tribe was it included?

Pupil. Asshur.

Monitor. For what was it remarkable?

Pupil. Commercial prosperity.

Monitor. In what class of powers should we place it?

Pupil. Naval.

Monitor. Was the second Tyre ever taken?

Pupil. Yes.

Monitor. By whom?

Pupil. Alexander the Great.

Monitor. Cite a passage of Scripture relating to that event?

Pupil. Isaiah xxiii.

Monitor. What is Tyre now?

Pupil. A place resorted to by fishermen to dry their nets.

Monitor. The prophecy respecting this?

Pupil. Ezekiel xxvi. 14.''

And so on, till Ezekiel, Isaiah, Alexander and Nebuchadnezzar were exhausted.

In the thirties, and still more in the forties, an attempt was made to relax the strict reference of all knowledge in the Lancasterian Schools to the Scriptures, and though no language was taught, ample explanations were given of the roots of words. This was probably not unconnected with the fact noticed by Kay-Shuttleworth: ''Those who have had close intercourse with the labouring classes well know with what difficulty they comprehend words not of a Saxon origin, and how frequently addresses to them are unintelligible from the continual use of terms of a Latin or Greek derivation. . . .'' A short illustration will show how it was attempted to make these words intelligible. In the highest divisions of the school, reading-books containing varied subjects, including ''general history, physics, and natural history,''

had been introduced. A lesson on natural history would
be given thus. The boys would read: "Ruminating
animals. Cud-chewing or ruminating animals form the
eighth order. These, with the exception of the camel,
have no cutting teeth in the upper jaw, but their place is
supplied with a hard pad. In the lower jaw there are
eight cutters; the tearers, in general, are absent, so that
there is a vacant space between the cutters and grinders.
The latter are very broad, and are kept rough and fit for
grinding the vegetable food on which these animals live,
by the enamel being disposed in crescent-shaped ridges."
And so on for a long time. Interrogation on this lesson
would then take place:

"*Monitor.* What have you been reading about?
   Boy. Ruminating animals.
   Monitor. Another name for ruminating?
   Boy. Cud-chewing.
   Monitor. What is the root of the word?
   Boy. 'Rumen,' the cud.
   Monitor. What does the termination *ate* mean?
   Boy. To do or act on in some way.
   Monitor. Ruminate, then, is to——?
   Boy. To act on the cud,"

and so on. And later:

"*Monitor.* You read in the lesson *the enamel is dis-
      posed in crescent-shaped ridges.* What is the enamel?
   Boy. The hard, shining part of the tooth.
   Monitor. What part of our tooth is it?
   Boy. The covering of that part that is out of the jaw-
      bone.
   Monitor. What do you mean by disposed?
   Boy. Placed.
   Monitor. The root?
   Boy. 'Pono,' I place.
   Monitor. What is crescent-shaped?

Boy. Shaped like the moon before it is a half-moon.

Monitor. Draw a crescent. (*Boys draw it on the black-board.*)

Monitor. What is the root of the word?

Boy. 'Cresco,' I grow,'' etc., etc., etc.

It is not remarkable to read in a footnote, ''At this point it would be necessary for the monitor to put many of these questions over again, to ascertain that there has been perfect comprehension of the subject.''

Possibly during his school years the boy's parents would move house, and it would be more convenient to send him to a school under the auspices of the National Society for Promoting the Education of the Poor in the Principles of the Established Church. He would probably have noticed little difference. The forms would be arranged differently, but he would still be taught by monitors or teach others as a monitor. The repertory of religious instruction would be enlarged; he would hear a good deal about something called doctrines; in place of continual ''catechetical interrogation'' on the text of the Bible, he would now learn to repeat the creeds and the catechism, whilst words like ''justification'' and ''sanctification'' would loom large on his horizon. If he stayed long enough at school, he might know less about the connexion of Tyre with Nebuchadnezzar and Alexander than if he had stopped at the Lancasterian School, but on the other hand he might hope to rival the class of children, aged ten to fourteen, described by Bishop Blomfield, who passed an excellent examination in the first nine chapters of Romans, explaining any passage on which they were questioned, and referring readily to parallel passages, and this in addition to showing knowledge of ''almost all the principal facts connected with the history of the New Testament, the application of the leading prophecies, and the common geography of the Holy Land.''

On leaving school the boy we have tried to describe

might not be altogether clear in his head about the doctrine of redemption and sanctification, or the pomps and vanities of the world, but he would have been still more puzzled to explain the declaration of the National Society whose school he had been attending, that they would not "timorously, unwisely, and supinely . . . give up into the Hands of our Enemies that sacred and victorious weapon, which we have so long and successfully wielded in the Defence and Preservation of the Religion, the Virtue, the Welfare and Happiness of our Country." To understand it he would have had to know something of the history of education during the preceding thirty years. That history would have made him aware that all the while, over the unsuspecting heads of the little boys and girls in the "Society" schools who were busy spelling out "The way of God is a good way," or "Bad men are foes to God," or adding up the children produced by Jacob's various wives, a battle was raging among the Olympians for the possession of their young souls. A brief sketch of that battle is essential if we are to understand the state of education when public help was first given to it.

At the end of the eighteenth and beginning of the nineteenth centuries, in the age of mechanical inventions, two remarkable men, Dr. Andrew Bell, a Church of England clergyman, and Joseph Lancaster, a Quaker, invented separately new and similar systems of teaching. Both discovered that education could be greatly cheapened by the employment of child labour; schoolmasters, except as heads, were superfluous; scholars could be used to teach each other. For the credit of this discovery there was fierce controversy between the partisans of the two men. Lancaster began his teaching career in London: Bell started his system as a chaplain in Madras, and hence it was often called the "Madras system." Never have educationists or their friends made higher claims. Lancaster, who announced that he had "invented, under the blessing of Divine Providence,

a new and mechanical system of Education," showed
that one master "might conduct a school of 1,000 children with perfect ease." Bell, who had a lively fancy,
though he did not mention the figure of a thousand, was
no less sanguine. "On this principle a superior can conduct any institution, how numerous soever, through the
instrumentality of its own members. In a school it gives
to the master the hundred eyes of Argus, the hundred
hands of Briareus, and the wings of Mercury. In other
words, by multiplying his ministers at pleasure it gives
to him indefinite powers, and enables him to instruct as
many pupils as any school will contain. While it bears a
manifest analogy to the mechanical powers, it infinitely
surpasses them in simplicity, economy, force, and effect.
With great propriety it has been called the STEAM ENGINE
of the MORAL WORLD. The intellectual machinery costs
nothing, grows in force and efficiency, by the use that is
made of it, and with the work which it has to perform:
viresque acquirit eundo. In a word, it is the *lever* of
Archimedes transferred from matter to mind." Nor were
his adherents less enthusiastic in their language. "If we
do not reproach the philosophers of old time with the
ignorance of what a Newton saw and investigated, we
must not find fault with those good men for not having
forestalled the merits and anticipated the discoveries of
a Bell," said the Dean of Chichester of those who had
tried to educate the young in the past. The new arrangement of the school-room seemed indeed to make it
possible to educate a large number of children at a small
expense. "Suppose," wrote Bell, "that in two empires
consisting each of 2,000,000 children to be educated, the
one on the old plan, in schools of 50 pupils each, the
other on the new, of 500, at the stipend of £50 to each
master. The amount of school fees, in the one case,
would be £1 a scholar, or £2,000,000; in the other, 2s. a
scholar, or £200,000—the difference being £1,800,000.
But, allowing the Madras master double this stipend, the
difference would then be £1,600,000."

Enthusiasts for education grouped themselves behind the two men according to their colour, and societies were founded to promote their respective principles. The Lancasterian Society (1808), afterwards called the British and Foreign School Society (1814), was unsectarian, and drew its main support from Whigs and Nonconformists. In its schools the Bible was taught without comment. The Society which followed Dr. Bell was called "The National Society for Promoting the Education of the Poor in the Principles of the Established Church," and taught Church doctrines as well as the Scriptures. The National Society, in addition to its enthusiasts, harnessed to its purposes a good many who had before been lukewarm, if not hostile, to scattering schooling wholesale. William Cotton, the philanthropist, giving evidence on behalf of the National Society, summed the matter up very justly, when he said that whilst the main supporters and real workers (of the National Society) were quite unaffected by any question of rivalry, yet "the success of Joseph Lancaster created a considerable sensation among those who were not very friendly to the education of the poor, but who would rather see the people educated by the National Church than by Joseph Lancaster, I readily admit." However this may be, and whatever the motives of its subscribers, the National Society was the wealthier of the two.

Let us now consider the position of education for the working classes when the Reformed Parliament began to sit in 1833. Whitbread in 1807, and after him Brougham, had pressed in vain for some scheme of national education. A large number of the existing schools were still (specially in towns) affairs of private enterprise. The extent to which the working classes in the industrial towns were supporting schools out of their pockets has perhaps been overlooked. In Manchester, for 4,070 children attending schools that were either free or partially assisted, there were 13,108 children attending entirely self-supporting schools. In Bury, the proportions were

652 to 1,799. In Salford, 1,950 to 3,709. In Birmingham 4,066 to 8,248. In West Bromwich, 423 to 1,131. In York, where there were many endowments, the figures were reversed, for there were 2,697 free and assisted scholars to 1,294 in self-supporting schools. In Bristol and Liverpool, too, there was a small majority of free and assisted scholars. In Bristol, the figures were 7,207 to 6,494; in Liverpool, 13,000 to 12,000. If the facts elicited by the Manchester Statistical Society about Rutland may be taken as typical, there was a majority in country districts of free and assisted scholars; in Rutland the figures were 1,610 to 1,218. The payments at the self-supporting schools in all the places investigated were much the same; 3d. to 4d. was usual at Dame Schools, 8d. to 9d. at the Common Day Schools. The Bristol Statistical Society made the interesting calculation that in that town, out of a population of some 120,000, working-class parents were paying no less than £15,202 19s. 6d. for the education of their children, that is, more than half the total parliamentary grant.

Important though these self-supporting schools were, public interest was centred on the work and the rivalries of the two Societies. That there was a lamentable deficiency in means of education was generally agreed; the full extent of that deficiency was a matter of guesswork. An ambitious attempt to clear the ground before action was made early in the new Parliament by Lord Kerry, who asked (May 24, 1833) for a return, which amounted to an educational census. Rickman, who had achieved brilliant results with the population returns, took it in hand, unpaid. The answers to the 15,000 circulars, enclosing elaborate schedules, sent out to overseers, were remarkably numerous and full. From this portentous mass of information, published in three volumes, it was calculated that out of an estimated population for England and Wales of 14,400,000, 1,276,947 children, or 1 in 11 of the population, were attending day-schools of some sort or other, whilst 1,548,890, or 1 in 9 of the population, were attending Sunday-schools. Unfortunately, although the returns were numerous and full, they were found on more careful investigation to be hopelessly incorrect. As an example, the Manchester Statistical Society found that in Manchester, where the total school-going population was about 18,500, allowing for certain mistakes which cancelled each other, the Kerry returns omitted 181 schools with 8,646 scholars. The truth was that the attempt was too ambitious. The experiences of the Manchester investigator throw light on the errors. At York, the masters of the Endowed and Charity Schools "answered all interrogations with the utmost caution and in the vaguest manner," each seeming to think that his own school could be omitted without affecting the accuracy of the total. At Salford, many of the mistresses, with a caution for which one cannot blame them, asked a "prudent neighbour" to come in before answering the questions. If *viva voce* questions were bad, elaborate schedules were worse. Apart from the universal dislike of filling up forms, detailed knowledge of the Scriptures had persuaded some that counting numbers was unlucky. "No, no," said one teacher, "you shan't catch me counting; see what a pretty mess David made of it when he counted the children of Israel."

Whilst the Kerry papers were being sent out the Government took two important steps. In the first place, they included in their Factory Act of 1833 provisions for the compulsory education of factory children. On paper every child was obliged to attend school for two hours a day, and if a suitable school was wanting, the Inspector was "authorized to establish or procure the establishment of such schools." As, however, no funds were provided, and as the relevant sections were carelessly drafted, these well-intentioned provisions were often a dead-letter, and, where carried out conscientiously by employers, were a tax on industry. The second step taken by the Government was to make a grant in aid of education. Their plan avoided the pitfalls of religious controversy. They gave £20,000 to be divided between the two Societies, in aid of subscriptions for building schools.

In the course of the next five years a good deal of light was thrown on the state of popular education in the reports of three Parliamentary Committees. The evidence given before these committees showed clearly that the most serious evil was the lack of effective provision for training teachers. The National Society took young men and women at the age of twenty-one onwards and gave them five months' training. Most of them had tried other professions or callings; some had come from "very respectable situations in life in which they have not been successful." The British and Foreign Society took them from nineteen years old to twenty-three or twenty-four. Their candidates were mostly ex-mechanics who had acquired a taste for teaching by helping in Sunday-schools. If they kept any of that taste after the three months' intensive training that was given them, they must have been remarkable persons. "Our object," said the Secretary, "is to keep them incessantly employed from five in the morning until nine or ten at night. We have rather exceeded in the time devoted to study the limit we would choose, on account of the very short period we are able to keep them, and we have found in some instances that their health has suffered on account of their having been previously quite unaccustomed to mental occupations." The future schoolmistresses seem to have stood the training even less successfully.

In 1839, Lord John Russell made a serious effort to meet this need. He set up by Order in Council a Committee of the Privy Council, consisting of four Cabinet Ministers, to superintend the application of the Parliamentary grants to education, with a Secretary and two Inspectors, who were to disseminate a knowledge of improvements among those engaged in education and to keep the Committee informed of progress. Dr. Kay, afterwards better known as Sir James Kay-Shuttleworth, was the first Secretary. He was a great public servant of independent mind and enlightened ideas, of whom Sir Michael Sadler has said: "To him more than to anyone else we owe it that England is supplied with schools for the children of her people, and that this costly work has been accomplished without a breach between Church and State."

Part of the Government scheme was the establishment of a Government Normal School for training teachers, and a Model School in connexion with it. This proposal caused a storm. The Church was outraged because in the Model School, attached to the Normal School, religious instruction was divided into "general" and "special," and the special instruction might be given, if desired, by Dissenting ministers. The candidate teachers in the Normal School could also have their special religious instruction provided from Nonconformist sources. This was taken to foreshadow a general "right of entry" into all schools. Nor were certain Nonconformists any better pleased. In the regulation that "either at the time fixed for reading the Scriptures, or at the hours of special instruction," Roman Catholics might read their own version of the Bible, the Wesleyan Methodists saw the triumph of the Scarlet Woman. This recognition by the State of "the corrupted Romish translations" they declared to be "a direct violation of the first principles of our Protestant Constitution."

The Government, to use Lord John Russell's expression, threw the Normal School to the wolves. The wolves tore the corpse and called for fresh victims. In a vigorous debate on the order for a Committee of Supply on June 14, adjourned till June 19 and 20, Lord Stanley, declaring that "education was the peculiar province of the clergy and was a spiritual matter to be entrusted to their superintendence," demanded the rescinding of the Order of the Council. Statistics, always a special feature of debates on education, were hurled backwards and forwards with equal effect to prove opposite conclusions. Prisons and penitentiaries were ransacked to show that education cured or encouraged crime. In the end the Government only escaped defeat by five votes (280 to 275). Four days later, when Lord John Russell moved the vote of £30,000 for education, the majority was still narrower, 275 to 273. In the Commons the Government had scraped through and had saved the grant by two votes; in the Lords, faced with episcopal rhetoric, they could not avoid censure. The Archbishop of Canterbury (July 5) proposed and carried a series of resolutions drawn up by Peel deprecating the Government's action, and proposing to present an address to Her Majesty to ask that no plan for general education should be established without consulting the House of Lords. Her Majesty was not sympathetic.

The Government had won a victory of a kind, but the Church had other weapons at her command. By the new arrangements grants carried with them the right of inspection. Against this the National Society protested vigorously. They began to refuse the grants, and, as the new Education Committee of the Privy Council existed to distribute public money, the boycott was serious. The question was settled in the summer of 1840 by the virtual capitulation of the Government. The Archbishops were given, not only a veto on the appointment of inspectors of Church of England schools, but also the power of discharging them at any time.

In 1839 the Whig Government had only saved itself by throwing important limbs to the wolves of the Church; in 1843 when the next attempt was made to improve education, this time by a Conservative Government, the wolves of Dissent claimed and obtained the whole corpse. Yet the proposals were made in one respect under favourable conditions. The riots of 1842 had caused general alarm, it was generally acknowledged that an ignorant populace was a dangerous populace, and Ashley, taking advantage of this mood, had carried a resolution in the House of Commons on the need for popular education. Sir James Graham in reply lamented that England had failed to profit by the warning of the French Revolution which might have taught the sects to moderate their quarrels. His new proposals were part of a Factory Bill, and meant in the first instance for factory children, but he hoped that the new schools would provide education for all children in factory districts. But his schools never came to life. The Nonconformists raised a storm, objecting partly because they thought the Church was given too much power in the management of the schools, and partly because the Sunday-schools might suffer. Graham went far to meet these objections, but the Nonconformists did not relax their hostility and he had to drop the scheme. He could have carried it through Parliament, but he might have been met by passive resistance when the schools were set up. Brougham described the position: "The Church was anxious to educate the people, but the Church was still more anxious to get the better of the sects; the sects were anxious to have popular education, but the sects were still more anxious than this to overturn the Church."

In July 1846 the Whigs again came into power, and the insistent Kay-Shuttleworth pressed his reforms with fresh ardour. Statistics about illiteracy were beginning to alarm politicians. Each year since 1839 the Registrar-General had given the number of married persons who signed with a mark. This percentage had remained practically unchanged. It had been 41·6 in 1839 (men, 33·7; women, 49·5), it remained at from 40 to 41·4 during the next six years. Yet schools had undoubtedly increased during the school years of the brides and bridegrooms. No time was lost. In August an outline of the new proposals was issued, followed in December by further details. The proposals, embodied in Minutes, consisted of an elaborate scheme for the reorganization of school teaching, and the improvement of the teachers'

position. Monitors were to be replaced wherever possible
by pupil teachers, apprenticed for five years. Grants
were to be given to the pupil teachers and to the teachers
who trained them. When the apprenticeship was finished,
the further training of the pupil teachers for three years
at a normal school was to be encouraged by a system of
scholarships and grants. Teachers thus trained were to
enjoy certain additions to their salaries provided by
grants, and retiring pensions were to be given under
certain conditions. The establishment of the pupil
teacher system in a school, and the additions to salaries,
were dependent on a favourable report from an inspector, and it was an inspector who conducted each
year the examination of the pupil teachers. Thus the
Education Committee for the first time obtained a
certain control over the schools it inspected and subsi-
dized. The qualifications of the pupil teachers for giving
religious instruction were to be tested in Church Schools
by the inspector, with the assistance of the parochial
clergyman; in other schools the managers were merely
required to certify that they were satisfied with the
candidates' religious knowledge.

These proposals were not an attempt to grasp English
education and remould it into a national scheme. No
Government was likely to try its hand at that for some
time. They were a scheme for improving existing schools
without altering the existing basis.

The Nonconformists again attacked the scheme, this
time with the support of Bright, who had just entered
Parliament and tried to answer Macaulay's argument
that it was the duty of the State to educate the people.
Fortunately Bright's view, that it was better to leave the
nation to such arrangements as we have described rather
than run the risk of increasing the influence of the
Church, was so completely discredited by the facts that
had been made public that the Government had no
difficulty in holding to their plan, though Macaulay lost
his seat in consequence.

If we leave the warring sects and politicians and come down to the small boys and girls for whose souls they fought, what changes do we find? The self-supporting Dame Schools and Common Day Schools were dwindling in number, and the Denominational Schools were increasing. Manchester afforded an extreme example of this change. Whereas in 1834–35 there were some 409 Dame and Common Day Schools with 11,512 scholars, in 1852 there were only 126 of these schools with 4,334 scholars. The children at National, British and Denominational Schools meanwhile had gone up from 3,818 to 15,270. But the private schools died hard. Judging from descriptions given later to the 1861 Commission on Popular Education, the character of these schools remained much what it was in the thirties. One is tempted, however, to think that the school mentioned where the kitten "to which all the children were very attentive" was the chief text-book may have given a better education than some schools where the Bible took its place. Most of our knowledge about schools in the forties comes from inspectors' reports, and these, of course, deal mainly with the grant-aided Church or Society Schools. Now it would be possible to pick out things said of these schools by the inspectors as harsh as anything said of the Common "Adventure" Schools by the Manchester Statistical Society, but we must not assume that they were worse than they had been; probably they were a good deal better. The truth was that the inspectors were the first people who discovered that a fog enveloped the children's minds, and that it was possible to read intelligently and even to answer questions correctly without having the slightest notion of the meaning of the words uttered. Any deviation from routine produced chaos. Mr. Tremenheere, examining the British Schools, put his questions in unexpected order:

"Q. Who were the Gentiles?—A. People of God.
Q. Who was Moses?—A. Apostle of Christ.

Q. Who was Peter?—*A.* An angel.

Q. Where was Christ crucified?—*A.* England.

Q. Who was Jesus Christ the son of?—*A.* Son of David.

Q. Who then was David?—*A.* Son of Jesus.''

The National Schools with their catechism provided equally striking examples.

''*Q.* Who gave you the name which you received in baptism?—*A.* God.

Q. What did your godfathers and godmothers promise and vow for you respecting the pomps and vanities of the world?—*A.* All the sinful lusts of the flesh.

Q. I asked what they promised and vowed respecting the pomps of the world?—*A.* That I should believe all the articles of the Christian faith.

Q. What do you mean by those articles?—(Silence.) The articles of the faith mean all the truths of the gospel; will you tell me any one of the truths of the gospel which your godfathers vowed you should believe? —Five were silent, the sixth answered, 'The Commandments.' ''

But though the children might seem to have lapsed into what Mr. Moseley, the inspector with perhaps the most vivid pen, called ''that vagrant state of mind, approaching to idiocy,'' yet, if appropriately handled, they could perform feats at the public examinations held before admiring subscribers, causing the audience, in the same inspector's bitter words, to ''go away with the impression that the children of the poor are receiving a better education than they did themselves.'' The feats of etymology or mental arithmetic were ''wonderful only as long as the short methods used in producing them are unknown.'' Etymology itself he described as a method of ''directing their attention to the derivation of one language, with which they are comparatively unacquainted, from another, of which they are profoundly ignorant.''

The severest indictment of the elementary education of this time was made, not by the school inspectors, but by the Children's Employment Commission in their Second Report of 1843 (p. 202). ''In all the districts,'' they stated, ''many children who had been returned as able to read, when examined were found to know only the letters of the alphabet; a very small proportion indeed being able to read well an easy book. Even of those who could read fluently, very few, when questioned, were found to have any conception of the meaning of the words they uttered, or were able to give any intelligible account of what seemed to the examiners to be simple and easy terms and things; so that, as far as regards the acquisition of any useful knowledge, or the accomplishment of any higher purpose to be answered by education, these Children, in great numbers of instances, were as little benefited, after years of so-called tuition, as if they had never been at any school.'' Mr. Moseley in 1845 calculated that out of the 11,782 children covered by his inspection, some 75 per cent would leave school unable ''to read the Scriptures with tolerable ease or correctness.'' Mr. Watkins reported in 1846 that out of 15,466 children in the schools he visited, a little under half were in the elementary stages of learning to read, whilst about a quarter could read simple narratives, and a quarter could read with ease. When we remember the short time spent at school it seems remarkable that the percentage of illiteracy was so low.

From one aspect it is fortunate that these schools housed a fleeting population. Lyon Playfair, writing of the Lancashire schools, says in the Health of Towns Commission Report, ''It is by no means an uncommon thing, on entering public schools, to observe children carried out in a fainting state, and the visitor, who feels the contaminated state of the air on entering it from a purer atmosphere, cannot be astonished at the occurrence.''

A detailed examination of the state of the schools brings out the importance of the Minutes of 1846. The pupil teacher system has an ugly sound in the ears of a generation unacquainted with monitors. The reforms of 1846 recognized, however imperfect their plan and methods, that the great discovery for which Bell and Lancaster disputed the credit, the discovery that children could be taught cheaply, had been a curse to education. The Government now set themselves with slow and feeble steps to the task of training efficient teachers, and creating efficient schools.

Though the education of children excited so absorbing a controversy, the education of adults was not altogether neglected. In practically every town of any size an intelligent workman who wanted to improve and educate himself would find by the forties a Mechanics' Institution, or some similar society. In England, in 1850, it was estimated that there were seven hundred of these societies with 107,000 members. The libraries connected with them contained over 690,000 books. But though the figures sound impressive, these institutions caused much searching of heart. They had failed to fulfil the expectations of their founders. Their rate of mortality was high, though their birth-rate was also high, and even in those that were comfortably established the membership was apt to fluctuate with alarming rapidity. To understand their position, it is necessary to glance back at their origins.

These institutions were started by Brougham and Birkbeck in the twenties at a time when, as a writer described it, ''there still prevailed in many quarters a strong jealousy of any political discussion by the people, and still more of any society which proposed to assemble periodically several hundreds of the labouring classes.'' Hence their founders, in their desire to conciliate opposition, banned political or religious discussion or books, and forbade newspapers. Even so, the *St. James' Chronicle* could say of the London Mechanics' Institution in 1825, "A scheme more completely adapted for the destruction of this empire could not have been invented by the author of evil himself than that which the depraved ambition of some men, the vanity of others, and the supineness of a third and more important class, has so nearly perfected." Even their advocates felt a certain need for apology: "I am at a loss," said Sir Benjamin Heywood, President of the Manchester Mechanics' Institution, in 1827, "to see how we are disturbing the proper station of the working classes, and giving them an undue elevation; we do not alter their relative position; a spirit of intellectual activity, unequalled in any age or country, now prevails amongst us, and, if the superstructure be renewed and strengthened, it does not seem fitting that the foundation should be neglected."

Mechanics' Institutions were established in the hope of popularizing scientific knowledge, and incidentally making the workman better at his work. The latter motive at first received the chief emphasis. At Manchester, for example, the preamble declared that "This society was formed for the purpose of enabling Mechanics and Artizans of whatever trade they may be, to become acquainted with such branches of science as are of practical application in the exercise of that trade, that they may possess a more thorough knowledge of their business, acquire a greater degree of skill in the practice of it, and be qualified to make improvements and even new inventions in the Arts which they respectively profess." It was a time when there seemed no limit to the possibilities of scientific and mechanical discoveries, and it was hoped that the new institutions might benefit not only their members but science itself by "uniting and concentrating the scattered rays of genius, which might otherwise be dissipated and lost to the scientific world."

Mechanics' Institutions had the difficult task of providing instruction for students on very different levels of book learning. Many members could not even read or write. Hence the Institutions had not only to spread scientific truth, but to act as glorified evening elementary schools as well, with classes for reading, writing, and arithmetic. They provided courses of lectures, classes of various kinds, and libraries, with reading-rooms often attached to them. But when the first excitement and enthusiasm had worn off, numbers dwindled in an alarming manner. The cult of the lecture soon languished. "After the first novelty of listening to lectures is over, the workmen can rarely be induced to attend them," wrote a disillusioned observer in 1839. It was discovered that the topic of the steam engine roused no enthusiasm in manufacturing districts. "The jaded artisan," explained John Cleave in 1842, "needs some relaxation after the severe privations and enervating toils of the day, and however much he may desire scientific lore, will turn with disgust from the necessary instruction, if presented in a mere dry and detailed form, ungarnished by a palatable admixture of the lighter mental food of general literature." A correspondent of the *Poor Man's Guardian* put it more bluntly: "Many of us are already saturated with as much of what is called science as we can carry."

The art of popular lecturing was in its infancy, and, as a successful lecturer on non-scientific subjects to Mechanics' Institutions expressed it in 1849, "A man must have a very happy talent for lecturing if he succeeds in making scientific lectures popular." Let us imagine a workman, eager to know the secrets of the new balloons, attending Mr. Tatum's first lecture on *Aerostation* at the London Mechanics' Institution. This is what he would be told at the outset. "Before the principles of *Aerostation* could be properly comprehended, a knowledge of *Pneumatics* was requisite; and he had a right to presume, from the lectures which had been delivered on that subject, that the Members were acquainted with the nature and properties of *air*. A knowledge of *hydrostatics* is also essential to the study of a science which treats of bodies floating in a certain medium, by displacing a quantity of the fluid in which they float, equal in weight to the floating body. Besides this, it is necessary to know that *air* is a *gravitating medium*, and, therefore, not only *Pneumatics*, but *Hydrostatics* must be understood; so far, at least, as relates to the *specific gravities* of bodies. Chemistry also is necessary. . . ." It is not surprising that the workman was shy of the lecture-room, and that when he went there he preferred the lectures given by local men in language which he could understand.

In the places where numbers kept up, it was noticed that the members were no longer, as at first was the case, predominantly workmen; clerks and small craftsmen took their place. Enthusiasts could account for this by explaining that, thanks to the opportunities for improvement, members rose in the social scale, and the institution rose with them, but this was not the usual view. Hudson has an interesting description of the way in which middle-aged professional men, and heads of firms, invaded the Athenæums, ousting the young clerks for whom they were intended. The clerks, in their turn, anxious to avoid the society of "the governor," joined the Mechanics' Institutions, where "the warehouseman, the packer, the carter, and the mill-hand shun the society of the clerk and the foreman, and . . . in turn quit the Institution which was established expressly for them."

Attempts were made to improve the libraries at Mechanics' Institutions. These libraries, whose totals of books often sounded very imposing, suffered from being composed largely of gifts. A lecturer who had made a special study of the subject described them vividly: "Many of the books are gift books, turned out of people's shelves, and are never used, and old magazines of different kinds, so that, out of 1,000 volumes, perhaps there may be only 400 or 500 useful ones. The rest are, many of them, only annual registers and old religious magazines, that are never taken down from the shelves." Samuel Smiles, who was well acquainted with the Yorkshire Institutions, said much the same thing: "Many of the books in Mechanics' Institutions are very unattractive; many of those books, for instance, which are given by way of presents, are books which nobody would think of reading nowadays; a large proportion of them are dull, heavy books." He remarked truly that to make a library successful there must be money for buying fresh books. Fiction was now made an important feature of the libraries, and it was even complained of the various Manchester Mechanics' Institutions in 1849 that they were "in the hands of a party who buy amusing books, and those who are really disposed to improve themselves have no voice."

Mechanics' Institutions, then, useful though they were, failed to accomplish all that was expected of them. Their founders had overestimated the zeal for knowledge in the working classes. They pictured all workmen, or at any rate all skilled workmen, as craving for instruction, like the Birmingham men of whom a successful lecturer at Mechanics' Institutions spoke in 1849. "I have known men rise at five and work till eight for book money, and then go to their day's work." He could pick out, he said, five or six working men as amongst the most intelligent and best-read persons in Birmingham. "They are men who have wrestled it out." But the cold fact is that the passion for knowledge is not widely distributed in any class, and when sacrifices must be made to satisfy it, the distribution is narrower still. Before the Ten Hours Act, too, many factory workers must have been physically debarred from attending lectures or classes. That, considering the circumstances, a remarkable desire for knowledge existed, was shown not only in the attendance, such as it was, at the Mechanics' Institutions, but in the numbers of small

so-called Mutual Improvement Societies that sprang up,
some of them mushroom growths that soon died away,
others developing into organized societies. A few working men would meet regularly in the evenings "to improve themselves by mutual intercourse," and this sometimes led to the starting of regular classes. The Leeds
Mutual Improvement Society, started by four young
men in 1844, went through a stage when "reading,
writing, grammar, and arithmetic, were taught and
learned amidst rakes, and hoes, and broken flowerpots"
in an old garden house. By 1850 it was giving classes
on subjects including Discussion, Chemistry, and French
to eighty members, in extensive premises in a back yard
off Kirkgate. There was a special crop of these informal
and unpretentious gatherings in the northern counties in
1849 and 1850, largely, no doubt, as the result of the
Ten Hours Act. Even lectures of the right kind, given
by the right kind of man, could be a success, as was
shown by the case of Mr. Richardson, a self-educated
teacher, who for fifteen years, in 1850, had gone round
as a peripatetic lecturer on Science to the scattered
northern villages, where "the toiling mining population
of Durham and Northumberland proceed over the hills
in rain, sleet, and frost, that they may learn the great
truths which civilization has made manifest." He
lectured on Electricity, Pneumatics, etc., "travelling
day by day, by cart, by rail and by coach far from the
great towns and public highways, with his extensive and
beautiful electrical apparatus, valued at £500." "Somewhat provincial in his dialect, perfect as a manipulator,
and correct in his statements, he never fails to interest
and instruct."

The original hope that Mechanics' Institutions, once
established with help from benevolent persons, would
become self-supporting soon vanished. The system of
quarterly subscriptions, even when fixed at the low rate
of three shillings, as at Birmingham, was unpopular with
workmen. If the sum was raised the numbers fell off.

There were no endowments from pious founders and benefactors; living benefactors were essential and were often generous, but in addition there was a constant campaign to raise funds by means of bazaars, exhibitions, and soirées. Though the museums of stuffed natural-history specimens or models of machinery usually became neglected dust traps, instead of producing the intellectual elevation expected from them, a great appetite existed for temporary exhibitions. At Liverpool three exhibitions between 1840 and 1844 raised £5,000 for the Mechanics' Institution. Patent ice, cartoons, dissolving views, a panorama, evening concerts, and a diving-bell were among the attractions. It is clear that much of the energy that should have been spent on spreading education was devoted to these campaigns for raising funds.

It was complained that whilst working-class energy was spent liberally on efforts to make a success of "provident societies, trade societies, temperance societies, and the various political clubs that from time to time agitate the country, there is no evidence to show any of this spirit of proselytism in favour of Mechanics' Institutions." John Cleave answered that ill success was attributable, "not to the apathy of Working Men—but to their utter and just repugnance to institutions supported in a great measure by patronage and conducted by patronage." When we read in Hudson that "The lawned Divine, and the ermined Duke feel a pleasure in presiding over the festivals of the artizan and the day labourer," it is easy to understand that many artizans and day labourers preferred the small informal societies which they had created themselves, where the improvement was done by themselves and not by their betters. But when these small societies grew to any size, problems of finance became as acute as in the case of Mechanics' Institutions. Much gratuitous work was done, but premises had to be rented or maintained, teachers and lecturers of advanced subjects had to be paid, and the

fees that could be charged without discouraging membership seldom covered the cost. How narrow was the
margin even where the membership was satisfactory and
enthusiastic was shown by the position of the Ancoats
Lyceum in its flourishing days in 1841, when the income
had exceeded the expenditure, but the Directors were
warned that should they "take an injudicious step, such
as engaging a Lecturer who should prove a failure, for
three nights, at two guineas per night, this, with the
expense of printing, would exhaust the surplus, and
leave no attractions for the remainder of the quarter...."

In 1841 (March 11) it was proposed in the House of
Commons by Mr. Gillon that grants should be given to
Mechanics' Institutions. He pointed out that Oxford
and Cambridge received public money, and claimed the
same privilege for advanced education for working men.
Peel, then in opposition, blessed the project, but when
he came into office he found the difficulties too formidable. The episode of the Hullah classes was a warning
that any attempt to help adult education would involve
the Government that made it in all the quarrels that had
raged so fiercely over the education of children.

Hullah was a musician with a genius for teaching
music and inspiring others with his own enthusiasm,
whose powers Dr. Kay determined to enlist for English
education. Under the auspices of the Committee of
the Privy Council for Education, though without any
financial help from them, Hullah started a singing school
for schoolmasters at Exeter Hall in 1841, employing an
adaptation of M. Wilhem's methods which he had
studied in France. The success was extraordinary; the
classes were thrown open to the public, and in addition
to schoolmasters and mistresses, Sunday-school teachers,
mechanics, and shopkeepers trooped in. In 1842 over
3,000 persons were attending the classes held by Mr.
Hullah and his assistants, and it was estimated that
50,000 schoolchildren in London were being taught on
his method by teachers who had been trained in it.

Unfortunately at the request of the pupils, three other classes were formed for teaching writing, arithmetic, and linear drawing, on the synthetic method. This proved fatal. When Parliament was asked for a grant for these classes the Bishop of London said that though he had been one of the original subscribers to the Hullah classes, this recent development had alarmed him. Classes were being established in different subjects without provision for religious instruction. In this way you might even establish a normal school where no religion was taught. Peel was in favour of the grant and so were the Whigs, but he could not brave the frown of the Church, and reluctantly he put the plan on one side. Adult education had to wait for half a century for aid from Parliament.

CHAPTER X

THE REVOLT

FOR the first quarter of the nineteenth century working-class life was overshadowed by the Combination Acts. These Acts made combination criminal, and in this way gave a wider range to the laws against conspiracy. Their effect in restraining combination is evident from the large number of Trade Unions which came to life after their repeal in 1824. But the habit of resistance to misfortune or injustice is strong in the English character, and even while the Combination Acts made organization dangerous and difficult, Trade Unions were active and daring. They had leaders of courage and ability, like John Gast the shipwright and John Doherty the Irish cotton-spinner, and they could often disguise their character under the name of Friendly Societies.

We cannot in these pages describe the fortunes of the several working-class organizations of the time. Men and women combined together in various ways to improve their conditions, and the history of these different efforts is important, interesting, and instructive. But there are certain movements which possess a wider significance. Hope and discontent assume at times a more sweeping character, revealing a deeper emotion, a stronger tide of feeling and ambition. In the Doherty-Owenite campaign, lasting roughly for five years from the winter of 1829, and in the Chartist agitation, we see a revolt against a view of life, a protest against a general system. The discontent discussed in this book is the discontent that has this universal sound.

In the winter of 1829 John Doherty founded a General Union of Operative Spinners. Six months later, in July 1830, he launched the National Association for the Protection of Labour, with the *United Trades Co-operative*

Journal, changed later into *The Voice of the People,* as
its organ. The Association, which began, and continued
to flourish, mainly in the textile industries, spread
rapidly from Lancashire and Cheshire into the Midlands,
and, to some extent, into Yorkshire, and had amongst
its affiliated bodies (of which there were over 150)
societies from various trades—Pottery, Mining, Hat-
making, and Engineering amongst them. Unfortunately,
quarrels at the centre and difficulties of organization
weakened the Association, and early in 1832 Doherty
was devoting himself, not to Trades Union work, but
to Short Time agitation, and the now feeble N.A.P.L.
was awaiting dissolution. Separate Unions, however, big
and small, continued to exist and even to flourish. The
textile industries had given the first movement its start.
The builders now took their place with a Builders'
Union which, after winning a number of local victories,
established itself as the leading union in the country,
with a membership of 40,000 or more. At this juncture,
Robert Owen, who had returned in 1829 from the United
States where he had made an unsuccessful social experiment, came into touch with the Trade Union movement.
It was a great opportunity for a man with a gospel, for
the movement, alive with hope and ambition, was ready
to welcome a prophet with open arms. Owen put before
the scattered Trade Union world his new idea of a
system of productive co-operation by which capitalism
could be abolished. The Builders' Union, at its National
Conference or "Parliament" in Manchester in September 1833, accepted the whole gospel. From a programme that sought to redress grievances, to put down
abuses, and to improve conditions of employment, they
turned to a great scheme for reorganizing, and, indeed,
for taking over, the building industry by means of a
Grand National Guild under the direct control of the
Union.

The new ideas made rapid progress. Under Owen's
influence, at a congress of Co-operative Societies and

Trade Unions in London, in October 1833, a Grand
National Moral Union of the Productive Classes for
Establishing a New Moral World was formed, embracing
not only Trade Unions but Co-operative and Owenite
Societies as well. This unifying body was changed, so
far as the Trade Unions were concerned, into the famous
Grand National Consolidated Trades Union whose
formal constitution was passed at a meeting of Trade
Union delegates in London in February 1834.

The Grand National was believed, rightly or wrongly,
to have had over a million members. It embraced, besides the large, powerful Unions, classes like agricultural labourers and women workers for whom combination seemed impossible except under some unusual
stimulus of despair or excitement. "Industrious
Females" were to be organized wherever practicable.
It looked as if the whole working-class population,
bringing its hopes and its dreams and all its institutions
from the chapel to the benefit society, had enlisted under
a single flag. The Grand National Union was, in fact,
the revolt of the classes for whom the civilization described in earlier chapters had left unsatisfied certain
fundamental instincts of human nature.

But whilst the Grand National was extending its
boundaries, the opposing forces were preparing to fight.
It had against it a Government resting now (after the
Reform Bill of 1832) on the broad basis of property,
large and small, rather than on the narrow basis of
eighteenth-century privilege. It had against it a race of
employers, hard, successful, and combative. In the same
month (September 1833) in which the builders were
accepting Owen's ambitious programme, Melbourne, the
Home Secretary, was promising Government help to the
West Riding employers in their battle against the
Unions. In March 1834, he struck at the Grand
National's weakest point, and being as ruthless in
politics as he was gentle in manners, he struck one of
those blows which resound through the world and leave

their echoes for generations. His victims were agricultural labourers, belonging to a county in which famine
and intimidation had brought man's spirit down to the
lowest level. Some agricultural labourers at Tolpuddle
in Dorset, hoping by the help of the Grand National to
raise their wages back from 7s. to 10s., formed a branch
of the Friendly Society of Agricultural Labourers, and
administered the oaths that were part of the ritual commonly followed on such occasions. But the use of this
ritual had been made a crime by laws passed in 1797
at the time of the mutiny of the Nore. Six men were
prosecuted, and being found guilty, as the *Annual
Register* (p. 39) describes it, "of swearing agricultural
labourers, and binding them to an observance of the
illegal oath, by ceremonies partaking of mingled folly,
superstition, and ferocity," they were transported for
seven years. Melbourne insisted on carrying out this
inhuman sentence, in spite of protests and entreaty,
showing himself one of those men who can be merciless
in cold blood when the hour of anxiety has passed. The
effect was immediate. The Grand National proceeded to
abolish the obnoxious oaths, but an organization so
loosely constructed was ill adapted to combat panic.
There was naturally more enthusiasm than efficiency at
the service of the movement, and it would have needed
no ordinary skill to organize this vast mass of hope and
faith into an orderly and disciplined army.

The Government had done its work. But the employers scarcely needed such aid. They fought and over-
came the movement in detail. Different sets of employers,
the builders in Derby, the hosiers in Leicester, the
clothiers in Leeds, all in turn offered their work-people
the choice of leaving their employment or signing a
document renouncing the Union. The Grand National
found itself in charge of a great and straggling battle-
field on which these hastily organized workmen were
pitted against men made inexorable by their self-con-
fidence and resolute by those stern qualities that had

carried them from poverty to wealth. For a struggle of this kind its resources were hopelessly inadequate. And as difficulty and disappointment came thick upon them, the several leaders inevitably became more and more conscious of each other's shortcomings. The Grand National stumbled along for a few months with dwindling strength, its last days embittered by all the distressing incidents that mark such defeats. But its failure does not obscure the significance of the birth and life of this movement. In a population whose economic condition, according to the statisticians, was better than that of their fathers and grandfathers, something like a million men and women had left the routine of their lives, made sacrifices, faced dangers, and suffered punishment to proclaim to the world that this improved condition left them acutely dissatisfied.

The revolt was inspired by men who had larger ideas than those of the ordinary Trade Union leader. This was true of Doherty, of Owen, and of the men who edited the papers of the cause. The working class was stirred by the belief that society might be radically changed; that life need not wear so hard and ungenerous a face; that the poor might have a share in the civilization of their age. The movement, then, is significant because of its scale, its character, and its ideas. It is remarkable also for something else. Its failure did not mark the end of the revolt. The Owenite revolt was followed by the revolt of Chartism.

The Charter itself was the product of the London Working Men's Association, a body of London Radicals among whom Lovett and Place were the leading figures. Francis Place, William Lovett, Henry Hetherington, and other Radicals had been brought together in a campaign against the Newspaper Stamp Duty. This duty, first imposed in the time of Queen Anne, and now standing at the high figure of fourpence, had been used by Castlereagh in order to strike at Cobbett and his fellow Radicals, for one of the Six Acts (1819) imposed this duty on all periodicals costing less than sixpence. It was hoped that the Whigs would repeal this duty, but they maintained it, and, as Radical editors refused to be silenced, there was a stiff struggle between journalists and the law. Between 1830 and 1836, 500 men were sent to prison for selling unstamped papers. The agitation was so far successful that the duty was reduced to a penny in 1836; it was not abolished till 1855.

In 1836 Place and Lovett co-operated in another enterprise. They formed the London Working Men's Association for discussing political reform. It was this body which drew up the Charter with its six points— manhood suffrage, ballot, annual parliaments, equal electoral districts, payment of members, and abolition of the property qualification for Parliament. Missionaries were sent out into the provinces, and this programme gradually drew together the different left-wing movements of the time, including the passionate agitation that had been provoked in the north by the new Poor Law. The Charter thus became the rallying flag for a number of different discontents, and much of the energy and spirit that had been collected for the Grand National was now brought into the service of the cause.

The history of the movement is confused and perplexing, because, though it had a definite programme with its six points, it embraced not merely divergent but mutually hostile schools of reform. We give the name of Chartist to the London artisan who shared Lovett's enthusiasm for education and a cheap press; to the Birmingham politician who supported Attwood's campaign for a reform of the currency; to the Lancashire handloom weaver or the Yorkshire collier who listened to Oastler denouncing the new Poor Law; to Feargus O'Connor, self-styled descendent of Irish Kings, spinning project after project from his active and ill-ordered brain, to the South Wales miner who followed Frost, with a pike, to Newport and to prison. Francis Place said on one occasion that the working man would not do anything even for his own advantage if that advantage were remote, and that he had no desire to stir himself for the advantage of other persons. Place hoped that education would produce a different temper. He referred to the education of the schools, but these men and women were learning in the school of life. For these movements show that men and women in their thousands were ready to follow any leader who promised them a radical change, whether he talked like Owen or Cobbett, like Oastler or O'Connor, whether he appealed to the ambitions of the trade unionist or the memories of the peasant, whether he offered to go forward or to go back, to build a golden future or recall a glittering past. For some ten years the English poor found in the Chartist agitation an opportunity of protesting against the place they occupied in the raw industrial settlements spreading over the Midlands and the North. This is the significance of the campaigns that began with the Convention of 1839 and ended nearly ten years later in the fiasco on Kennington Common.

The Charter itself was first published in May 1938. During the rest of the year successful mass meetings were being held all over the industrial districts with the object of uniting existing movements of discontent in a demand for the six points. The first step was to be the election of a People's Convention, which was to impress Parliament by presenting a monster Petition. For this purpose, Poor Law reformers, currency reformers, Radical reformers, sank their differences. Missionaries from the Working Men's Association in London, and Feargus O'Connor, with his powerful rhetoric and his powerful paper, the *Northern Star*, founded in November 1837, helped in the campaign.

In February 1839 a Convention of 53 delegates, chosen mainly from industrial centres at public meetings arranged by Chartist bodies, met in London in order to promote a monster Petition to Parliament for the Charter. Lovett was appointed Secretary. By May 5 the Great National Petition was ready, it was three miles long, contained 2,283,000 signatures, and was solemnly escorted to the house of Attwood by the Convention, marching two by two. Attwood was to present it to Parliament. Unfortunately, at the moment Parliament was not interested. On the day that the Petition reached Attwood, Melbourne's Government resigned, what is known as the Bedchamber crisis followed, and it was not till June 14, after the Whigs were re-established, that the Petition was presented, and not till July 12 that it was debated. Meanwhile it became clear that the walls of Jericho were not going to fall before any Petition, however huge. What was to be done? How was Parliament to be induced or forced to listen? What if they listened but rejected it? The Convention became absorbed in the discussion of tactics. Should physical force be used or moral force only? Though extremists at both ends, specially at the moderate end, had dropped off, agreement seemed impossible. On May 13 the Convention moved to Birmingham, where the surroundings were safer and more congenial than in unenthusiastic London, and continued the debate. They ended by adjourning for six weeks, till July 1, in the hopes that the country would give them a policy. First they issued a stirring manifesto, urging their countrymen not tamely to submit if the Charter were rejected, but to take "ulterior measures," and detailing these measures. They included a run on the Banks, a General Strike, the boycotting of non-Chartist shops, and the preparing of the "arms of freemen" to defend their laws and privileges.

When the Convention met again in Birmingham on July 1 no settled policy had emerged. They decided to move back again on the 10th to London, to be at hand during the Parliamentary debate. Before that date there were troubles at Birmingham, which damaged the position of the Convention. The Bull Ring, a favourite meeting-place during the Reform Bill agitation, was, naturally enough, used by the Chartists. Inflammatory speeches and unruly gatherings became common there, and the Magistrates prohibited all meetings. In the general excitement during the Convention's visit to Birmingham, on July 4, the Bull Ring was invaded again. The Mayor and magistrates in panic fetched 60 policemen from London and ordered them to disperse the crowd. There were ugly struggles and some damage to property. The Convention promptly published some vigorous resolutions protesting against the use of a "blood-thirsty and unconstitutional force," from London. Lovett, who, as Secretary, had signed the resolutions, and Collins, who had been Chairman when they were passed, were promptly arrested for seditious libel. (Several other Chartist leaders had by this time also been lodged in gaol.) The Convention did not modify their language, continuing to denounce "the Base, Brutal and Bloody Advisers" of Her Majesty, and moved back, as arranged, to London, to await the long-looked-for debate in Parliament. The debate roused little interest and no enthusiasm in the House. The speeches of the proposer and seconder, Attwood and Fielden, both of them hostile to the more violent proposals of Chartist policy, succeeded, says the *Annual Register*, in "eliciting some very sensible remarks from Lord John Russell"; Disraeli expressed sympathy, not for the Charter, but for the actors in this "very remarkable social movement," but only 46 Members voted that the Petition should be taken into consideration, as against 235. Hopes of Parliamentary action were dead.

The Convention had now to decide on action—or in-action. In reduced numbers (30) they met on July 15 for further discussion. After two days' debate they decided by 13 votes to 6 (with 5 abstentions) to decree a National Holiday, otherwise called a Sacred Month, or, less picturesquely, a General Strike, to start on August 12. But in a week they lost their nerve—perhaps they reflected on the growing number of workmen who had no employers to strike against—and they rescinded the order. Another serious Bull Ring riot had brought more discredit on the cause. The Convention had lost whatever powers of leadership they ever possessed, and in September they voted their own ignominious end.

All through the summer and autumn of 1839 the Chartist leaders, as well as their followers, were being thinned out. Local authorities, encouraged by Government, acted with vigour, Arrests for sedition, for unlawful meetings, for unlawful arms, grew common, whole batches of prisoners were occasionally tried. How far was there justification for the widespread expectation of an armed rising? Widespread it certainly was, not only in government and magisterial circles, but amongst Chartists themselves. To what did all the talk about pikes and using the arms of freemen amount? That there were no outbreaks of violence in the North, in spite of the enormous and excited meetings, was doubtless due to the conduct of Sir Charles James Napier, whom the Government set in command over the Northern counties. Napier, who was not only a very wise man but also more than half a Chartist himself, took infinite trouble to avoid a conflict, and the general respect in which he was held was a powerful influence on the side of peace.

Napier was very sceptical about the tales of organized rebellion. The fate of Frost's so-called rising in South Wales, when a Chartist army was rapidly routed by 28 soldiers, shows that whatever plans there might have been were completely futile. In this Newport rising large bodies of men, some said thousands, assembled outside the town on November 3, intending to enter it at night. Plans went wrong, and the main body under Frost, after wandering about for several hours, arrived in broad daylight. They came to the hotel where the soldiers were lodged and tried to force an entrance. The soldiers retaliated by sweeping the street with rifle fire, and in a few minutes the rioters were dispersed, leaving some 10 dead and about 50 wounded. What Frost's aim was it seems impossible to say, with certainty, in spite of the fact that he died in England at the age of 93, after being reprieved from the scaffold and enduring long years of transportation. The release of the Chartist Vincent from Monmouth gaol was generally supposed to have been his object. It has been suggested by Mr. Cole that Frost's rising may have been only one of a series of local riots in the thirties against the intolerable conditions in the iron and steel industries, in one of which the rioters had lost 15 dead and 60 wounded, but had succeeded in disarming some soldiers.

With the collapse of the Convention, the arrest of many leaders, and the much-advertised fiasco of this Newport affair, Chartism for a time sank below the surface. Even the hottest head could no longer think that the Charter would have been the law of the land within a month if the Convention had done its duty. For over two years the working classes were to resemble more closely those Spitalfields weavers who were once praised for congregating together in their multitudes "with so little inconvenience to their neighbours." Energies were spent at first in organizing petitions to save the lives of Frost and his two companions. They were largely signed and were successful. Plans for what O'Connor denounced as "Church Chartism, Teetotal Chartism, Knowledge Chartism, and Household Suffrage Chartism" were pursued. A new campaign for reorganizing the movement for the Charter itself began in the summer of 1840 and resulted in the formation of the National Charter Association. Lovett, released from prison in July, refused to take part in this, for he was devoting himself not to a direct demand for the Charter, but to a plan embodied in the "National Association for Promoting the Political and Social Improvement of the People," whereby the working classes were to educate themselves so successfully that their claim to the Charter would prove irresistible. By July 1841 the National

Charter Association was sufficiently well organised to take some part in the General Election, making trouble for the Whigs, and to arrange for a second Convention and a second Petition in 1842, thus repeating the procedure of 1839.

O'Connor was released from prison in August 1841, and added much vigour, though little wisdom, to the campaign. The National Charter Association was an active, hard-working body, full of enthusiasm, but its abundant members (100,000 were claimed) seem to have been chary of paying their subscriptions of 1d. a week. The new Convention was a smaller body than its predecessor, consisting of 24 members only, and it was to sit for four weeks only, thus avoiding unnecessary expense, and the long, useless discussions and quarrels indulged in by the earlier assembly. Even so, two whole days of its sittings were occupied by a motion urging Chartists to abstain from private slander and schism. The 1842 Petition was larger than its predecessor. It contained 3,317,702 signatures and was over six miles long, and when it had been carried to the House on May 2 by 30 bearers, followed by a procession, its framework was found to be so extensive that it had to be broken up before entry was possible. The debate about it, a lively one, took place next day, and was remarkable for Macaulay's denunciation of universal suffrage as "incompatible with the very existence of civilization" and for Roebuck's denunciation of O'Connor, in the course of a speech for the Charter, as a "fierce, malignant, and cowardly demagogue," a description which gave great pleasure to the opponents of the Petition. The motion that the petitioners should be heard was defeated by 287 votes to 49. In spite of the extra million signatures, only three more members had voted for it than for its predecessor, and there were 52 more votes against. Clearly there was no prospect of inducing the House to listen to the Chartists.

Whilst the National Charter Association were busy

with the second Petition, another movement for the same object was going ahead. Joseph Sturge, the Birmingham Radical Quaker, together with some of the Left Anti-Corn-Law Leaguers, started a campaign for complete suffrage. He appealed to working men to join in, and Lovett and some of the less extreme Chartists did their best to arrange a working alliance. Sturge's own ideas were not so far to the Left as were those of his Chartist associates, but at a Conference in April 1842, when a Complete Suffrage Union was established, all the six points of the Charter were adopted. In spite of some protests, the six points became six principles, and all mention of the Charter was carefully avoided. The question of the name was left over till the December meeting of the Union. The Complete Suffrage Union and the National Charter Association continued to work separately, and thus within two weeks of each other they were petitioning Parliament and obtaining debates on the same subject. The middle-class body had on April 21 presented a petition with only 40 signatures, trusting to quality rather than quantity, but obtained a less meagre proportion of votes: 67 to 226. Sturge stood as a Complete Suffrage Union candidate at a by-election for Nottingham in May 1842 against John Walter of *The Times,* and was supported even by O'Connor, who had before described his movement as "Complete Humbug." Sturge was only defeated by 34 votes, 1801 to 1835.

Before the Complete Suffrage Conference in December, at which the question of the name "Charter" was to be decided, the National Charter Association took a course which did not make the word any more acceptable. Trade was depressed, wages were reduced, unemployment increased; the new Poor Law was in working order, and the new Bastilles were ready to swallow up the unemployed. Twenty thousand Stalybridge weavers marched on Manchester; the movement spread rapidly, and soon gaunt, ragged, half-starved multitudes, armed with rough weapons, roamed about the North and Mid-lands, often pulling out the boiler plugs at the empty works, whence the name of the Plug Plot. It was a demonstration of mob violence against their employers. Many of the Chartists saw here an opportunity for pro-moting the Charter, and, in spite of some opposition, the National Charter Association issued a manifesto urging the strikers to avoid violence indeed, but to hold out until the Charter was won. The God of Justice and of Battle was called on for His help. Many of the strikers took up the cry, but the change of object produced neither food nor funds; troops were poured into the dis-ordered districts, and by the end of September the out-burst was over, the strikers were suing for work, and Chartism was inextricably mixed up with mob violence in the public mind.

The price to be paid for the outbreak was heavy. The Chartist manifesto was treated by the Government as a treasonable proclamation. Here, there, and everywhere, prominent Chartists were picked out and consigned to gaol. Special Commissions were appointed to deal with the rank and file as well. They sat in Lancashire, Cheshire, and Staffordshire. At Stafford the Commission transported 54 prisoners and imprisoned 154, all but 8 with hard labour; at Liverpool the Commission trans-ported 11 and imprisoned 115. Next year, 1843, fears of any Chartist rising must have passed away. It is difficult to explain otherwise the curious trials of a batch of prisoners at the Lancashire Assizes in March 1843, when 59 prominent Chartists, including O'Connor, charged with sedition, conspiracy, and unlawful assembly dur-ing the recent disorders, were all either acquitted, or else never called up for judgment, on the technical ground that the place where the offence was committed was never mentioned in the indictment.

Before the year 1842 ended, the alliance with Com-plete Suffrage was broken up. At the Conference in December, when the question of the name came up again, Lovett, supported by O'Connor, a strange fellowship, insisted that the word Charter, for which men had fought and suffered and died, must be retained and not be replaced by a mere "Bill of Rights." The motion was carried, but the alliance was wrecked, and the Complete Suffrage Union dragged out its life for a year or two without working-class support.

For the next few years Chartism as a fight for the Charter was moribund. Under O'Connor's autocratic rule a great Land Scheme was launched for improving conditions of industrial life by settling great bodies of workers back on the land in individual holdings of from one to four acres. It met with great enthusiasm from men and women longing to escape from the tyranny of factory life, and some £90,000 was subscribed by would-be smallholders. But the task of management and finance was a hopeless one, and O'Connor was a demagogue, not an administrator.

In 1848, under the stimulus of foreign revolutions, political Chartism raised its head again. There was some intercourse between the more violent-minded Chartists and Continental revolutionaries. Marx even assured the working men of England that, if only they succeeded in their fight for the Charter, they would be hailed as the saviours of the whole human race. The ordinary working man might know little about the Continent, but change and revolution were in the air, and tales of secret arming with the perennial pikes, as well as actual riots, became common. O'Connor, who had been elected for Nottingham in 1847, the first and the only Chartist Member of Parliament, now turned his attention back from the land panacea to the Charter. Undaunted by precedent, the Chartists arranged a third version of the proceedings of 1839 and 1842. There was to be a third Convention, of 49 members this time, and a third, even greater, monster Petition. The Convention met in April. Foreseeing the probable rejection of the Petition, they decided that a National Assembly must be convoked, to remain "permanently sitting" till the Charter was the law of the land. The Petition was said to contain not less than 5,706,000 signatures. The people in its majesty was to assemble on Kennington Common on April 10, and to march with the Petition to Parliament in a mighty procession, O'Connor at the head. The story of the disastrous anticlimax of that day is well known. Tales of the preparations had caused in Government circles and among the well-to-do classes in general a panic such as has been seldom known before, and never since. Troops were poured into London, the Duke of Wellington was put in command, 170,000 special constables were enlisted, among them Louis Napoleon, then a refugee, living in King Street. Before the procession started from Kennington, some police officials arrived and warned O'Connor that, in accordance with a law of the time of Charles II (resuscitated for the occasion) forbidding petitions to be presented by more than ten persons, the procession would not be allowed to cross the Thames. O'Connor, who had never intended violence to be used except in speech, meekly acquiesced, the monster Petition was taken quietly to the House of Commons over Blackfriars Bridge in three hansom cabs, and the crowds dispersed, not only without the expected bloodshed but without any serious disorder. The genuine alarm turned to merciless laughter when it was discovered by the Committee on Public Petitions that instead of the vaunted five million signatures there were just under two million, that many of these were preposterous, such as Victoria Rex, Duke of Wellington, No Cheese and Flatnose, and, a last touch of the ludicrous, that instead of the boasted five tons, the Petition weighed only five and a half hundredweight. The demonstration which had spread such alarm in anticipation left a legend of ridicule. Chartism as a gospel preached by a few valiant though quarrelsome champions lingered on for many years, but as a serious method of expressing industrial discontent it was thoroughly discredited.

It is natural that historians, with their imagination caught by the movements that made 1848 so lurid a memory for European government, should think lightly of a revolt that had so sober a career and so slight a casualty list. When we remember the slender provision for the maintenance of order (until 1839 neither Manchester nor Birmingham had a properly organized police force, and Bradford, with a population of 66,000, depended in the early forties on six constables), it seems extraordinary that more violence was not attempted, and that the Newport rising is an isolated incident. But disinclination for street-fighting did not mean that the Chartists were not in earnest, or that they were unready to run personal risks for their cause. The English workman is, and always has been, less ready to try violence than the workman of the Continent.

To regard Chartism as an episode, as an effort that failed, a flash in the pan, is to misread the history of the time. The chief feature of that history is the growth and prevalence of discontent. No doubt that discontent was due to different causes and fed from different sources: the discomforts of the change from the life of the peasant or the artisan to that of the factory worker; the pressure from time to time of mass unemployment unrelieved by any remedy; the special hardships of the new Poor Law. But if its general character is to be described, it was discontent excited by the philosophy of life, of which the new town was the symbol and the expression. "The political economists in Church and State," said the *Crisis*, "are the real high priests of the realm. They have set up the golden calf. . . . Impious, dissatisfied people, say they, you men without property, mob and scum of the earth, with minds born to inferiority and hands made for our service. Why, if you are still discontented, do you not seek to accumulate wealth and so become respectable like ourselves?" Instead of aiming at respectability, the workman was swept into one movement after another, as his imagina-

tion was captured first by this gospel, then by that. Any
man who could promise with golden tongue to lead him
out of his hard and desolate world became his leader.
"Every appeal," said Vincent, "to the intellect and
virtue of the masses is most cordially responded to."
The rulers of the new society had forgotten that if you
wish to satisfy a people you must satisfy its imagination:
the leaders of the revolt knew that if you want to rouse
a people you must rouse its imagination. The Chartist
movement, like Owen's movement, was imagination in
action. And when Chartism flickered out this force was
not lost. It went into different movements, like the
movement for education, the movement for public
health, the Trade Union movements, the movement for
temperance, and the later movements for the franchise.
Long after the great project of 1848 had collapsed amid
the relief and ridicule of London, the virtue of the
Chartist movement was by these means building up the
self-respect of the English workman. In this sense, as in
some others, Chartism deserved the phrase Mill applied
to it, the victory of the vanquished.

CHAPTER XI

THE DUEL OF LANDLORD AND MANUFACTURER, 1838–1847

It looked in the thirties as though English politics would be dominated for half a century by a passionate quarrel between rich and poor. This quarrel had broken out before 1832, and the Reform Bill seemed only to have made it more violent. As the *Chartist* put it: "The first use which a class always makes of its representation is to shift its burden upon somebody else's shoulders." The advent of the middle class to power was no exception to the rule. What was the gift of the Reform Parliament to the poor? The east wind of the new Poor Law.

If we look at the history of England between 1840 and 1890, we see that the conflict which seemed so imminent died away. There was less class war in the fifties than in the thirties. For this change there were two reasons, apart from the general improvement in the economic condition of the country: the class war was pacified by the influence of a general civilizing movement, which modified the sharp consequences of the Industrial Revolution, and it was distracted by another conflict between the landlord and the manufacturer, which determined the course of politics for the next ten years. The two agitations in which this quarrel found its outlet are the agitation for the Repeal of the Corn Laws and the agitation for the Ten Hours Bill.

The history of the Corn Laws in Parliament begins for our purposes with the passing of the Corn Law of 1815, prohibiting importation when the price was below 80s. a quarter. In 1828, Wellington set up a sliding scale beginning with a duty of 36s. 8d. at 50s., decreasing to 16s. 8d. at 68s., and 1s. at 73s. In 1841 the

Whigs proposed a fixed duty at 8s., but the dissolution of that year brought in Peel who carried a new sliding scale beginning with a 20s. duty at 51s., decreasing to 12s. at 60s., and 1s. at 73s., Russell and Melbourne being beaten in their efforts to substitute a fixed duty. So far the official policies of the Liberal and Conservative parties were Protection, by a fixed duty in the first case and by a sliding scale in the second, but all the time, of course, there had been an important body of opinion in Parliament in favour of dropping Protection altogether. In the Lords, men like Fitzwilliam, Brougham, Durham, and Holland had voted in favour of this policy in 1839; in the Commons, Villiers made annual motions for Repeal, being supported in 1842 by 90 votes, in 1843 by 125, and in 1844 by 124.

The organization which, with the help of famine, was to get rid of the Corn Laws, gained a victory as rapid as it was sensational, for it was only in September 1838 that the Anti-Corn-Law League was established. The League is famous in history, not merely because of its achievement, but because of its leaders, two men who were particularly powerful in combination. Cobden was a man with a large reflective mind, and an unrivalled gift for argument and exposition. Bright, a more combative man, apt in his earlier career to be bitter, rasping, and unfair, became a consummate master of a simple eloquence which was always telling and often beautiful.

To understand the effects of this agitation on the temper and imagination of the time, we must note certain facts about it. The Anti-Corn-Law League was organized and financed by a rich class with a remarkable capacity for propaganda and organization acquired in the world of business. It was able to employ expert writers and speakers all over the country. By 1842 the League had spent £100,000: in 1843 it raised £50,000: in 1844 it raised nearly £100,000 and was spending £1,000 a week. At a meeting of the League in Manchester in 1845, £60,000 was subscribed in an hour and a half. Such were the resources at the command of this agitation. They were put to most effective use. At a time when there was a rage for periodical literature, the League distributed nine million carefully argued tracts by means of a staff of eight hundred persons. The League had its organ, called at first the *Circular*, and afterwards the *League*. Meetings were held incessantly all over the country, and the League paid the Chartists the compliment of arranging conventions from time to time in the principal towns. Towards the end of the agitation the League discovered another weapon. The Reform Act of 1832 gave the county vote to the 40s. freeholder. The League set up an office to facilitate the purchase of freeholds in the county constituencies by free traders from the neighbouring towns, in the West Riding and Lancashire. If Repeal had not come in 1846, the same plan would have been applied in Middlesex and Surrey.

This agitation, led and financed by rich men, was so conducted as to draw poor men into its orbit. It was essentially popular in character. The Repeal of the Corn Laws was demanded in the interests of English industry, which suffered because exchange was impeded for the sake of English landowners. Under certain conditions a contest over the Corn Laws would have been a contest between industry and agriculture, between the townsman and the peasant. But the agrarian history of England, with the dispossession of the peasant and the degradation of the labourer, made it impossible for the struggle to assume such a complexion in English politics. No man, knowing the history of the English village for the last half-century, could persuade himself that the Corn Laws had brought anything but hunger to the mass of the village population. The poor, as *The Times* put it, deserted the landlords in this struggle, but then the landlords had first deserted the poor. Thus the campaign became a campaign against a rich class. The Repealers asserted more than once that they had concentrated on one question and put every other issue on one side. It would be truer to say that they had concentrated on one class, for the columns of the *League* were filled with the crimes of landlords and with denunciations of the game laws and other abuses of feudal power. The Repeal agitation was in certain aspects an agitation for an object of great importance to the industrial capitalists, and the subscription lists to its funds show how widely this truth was recognized. But it was at the same time an agitation pressing day after day the wrongs of the poor, and denouncing the selfishness of the rich.

The agitation was fiercely polemical. Even Cobden, who preferred argument to invective, gave the discussion the kind of tonic that politics demanded at this time, in such a passage as that in which he compared the landlords to the German nobles. "They had heard of the Union of Hanse Towns. Why did they unite? To put down aristocratic plunderers; and they would say to the aristocrats of England, Why do you plunder the beehives of Lancashire and Yorkshire?" *The Times* pointed out that one great difficulty about the Public Health agitation was that it never became violent, and therefore never became interesting. The movement for the Repeal of the Corn Laws was a fighting movement organized by a combative class. The *League* boasted in its farewell number that it was the only agitation in English history which had been founded and conducted exclusively by the middle classes. It had at its back men who were indignant about a general injustice, and not less indignant about a particular injustice, of which they thought themselves the victims. A movement, alive in this way with public and private anger, interested the English people from the first.

The agitation for the Repeal of the Corn Laws was thus an important force in distracting the class quarrel that had found its expression in Chartism, for it was, in one aspect at any rate, a quarrel with the rich on behalf of the poor. And it was a quarrel on an issue on which the workmen originally agreed with the Repealers. For the working classes were by tradition free traders on this question. The Corn Bill of 1815 had excited the most violent opposition. "The Repeal of the Corn Laws" was inscribed together with "Universal Suffrage" and "Annual Parliaments" on the flags that were carried to Peterloo. The early Chartist movement was not hostile to the Repeal movement; it was merely sceptical of its prospects and suspicious of its promoters. The *Chartist* wrote strongly in favour of Free Trade in February 1839 as the only way of saving England from the fate of Holland. In March the paper criticized the Corn Law repealers as 30 or 40 gentlemen representing themselves and their own breeches pockets, unlikely to make an impression on the selfishness of the landlords. In the same month it argued that the stubborn resistance of the House of Lords ought to convince the middle classes that Repeal was only to be obtained by combining with the Chartists. "Put a pike in a fishpond and he will eat up every roach and dace first, avoiding the perch because he has a sharp back fin which cuts his mouth: but when the roach and dace are all gone, and hunger presses, he attacks the perch and despite the fin back he soon makes an end of them." The Corn lords were the pike, the middle classes were the perch, and the working classes, the roach and dace, were already swallowed. A Free Trade paper, the *Morning Chronicle,* proposed an arrangement with the Chartists, who were to be offered household suffrage, but the *Chartist* rejected any idea of such a compromise. In 1842, as we have seen (see p. 183), there was an attempt to bring the movements together in the establishment of the Complete Suffrage Party, but the attempt failed and the two movements were forced into a violent quarrel, a quarrel in which Chartism suffered much more than Repeal. Feargus O'Connor could make a loud noise, but when it came to a contest the League could make a louder.

In 1845, when the Repeal agitation was at its height, came the shock of the Irish Potato Famine. Peel, faced

with a starving population and embarrassed by the
failure of the English harvest, saw that it was impossible
to maintain the law that kept food out of the country.
But if that law was suspended, could it be reimposed?
While Peel was hesitating, Lord John Russell wrote his
famous letter to the electors of the City of London
announcing his conversion to Repeal. In December Peel
proposed to his Cabinet to modify the Corn Law, and
resigned office because two of his colleagues, Stanley and
Buccleuch, dissented. Russell was asked to form a
Government, but he soon abandoned the task—
nominally because Howick would not join him if
Palmerston went to the Foreign Office; really because he
was not prepared for a battle with the Lords over Protection. Peel returned to office, introduced a Bill providing for the admission of corn at 1s. duty after
February 1, 1849, and carried it through Parliament in
the summer of 1846, by a majority of 98.

We must now turn to the agitation for the Ten Hours
Bill. The history of this agitation goes back to the first
Factory Act passed in 1802 by the elder Peel. This Act
limited the hours for apprentice children to twelve a day
for six days of the week. In 1819 Peel succeeded in
putting another Act on the Statute Book. This Act
much more modest than he wished, forbade the employment of children under nine in cotton mills and limited
the hours of children between nine and sixteen to twelve,
exclusive of meal hours. In 1831, John Cam Hobhouse,
who had succeeded in 1825 in reducing the Saturday
hours for children from twelve to nine, carried a Bill
extending the twelve hours' day to all persons under
eighteen. In 1831 Michael Sadler, a Tory M.P., introduced a Bill limiting hours in all mills for persons under
eighteen to ten. At the election of 1832 Sadler lost his
seat and Ashley took his place as parliamentary leader
of the cause, occupying in this agitation the place Villiers
occupied in the Repeal agitation. In 1833 he introduced
a Bill on Sadler's lines, but the Whig Government

amended it, improving it in one important respect, for inspection was introduced, but weakening it on its main principle, for whereas the hours for children under thirteen were to be limited to nine, the hours for persons between thirteen and eighteen were to be limited to twelve.

From this time the factory struggle was as much a struggle for a ten hours' day for all persons under eighteen as the struggle for amending the Corn Laws was a struggle for repealing them. You might amend the factory system without passing a Ten Hours Bill. The factory system was indeed amended and improved in detail before the Ten Hours Bill was passed. But, so far as popular agitation was concerned, the factory question was the ten hours' question and no other. The Ten Hours' Bill raised, in one sense, a complicated issue. It had become clear by this time that it was impossible so to organize the working arrangements of the mill as to combine a twelve hours' day for adults with a ten hours' day for persons under eighteen. A ten hours' day for persons under eighteen meant that the day for persons over eighteen would also be a ten hours' day. Parliament was therefore being asked to limit the hours for adults and not merely the hours for children, to limit the hours for the whole mill, not for one set of workers. This is what the workmen understood by factory reform.

The organization which conducted the campaign outside Parliament was a Central Short Time Committee (with branches in all the different towns) made up of trade unionists, of whom the most famous was John Doherty, and supporters from other classes, of whom the most important were Fielden, Wood, and Oastler, and the Rev. G. S. Bull. The Committee was poor in comparison with the League, which could draw on the help of manufacturers whose public spirit was encouraged by the prospect of commercial advantage. In this case the chief support came from manufacturers who stood to lose, if Peel and Cobden were correct in their estimate of the consequences of the Bill, for the six-pences and threepences of the mill-workers were supplemented by large subscriptions from manufacturers like Fielden and John Wood, the Bradford worsted spinner, who is said to have spent in all £40,000. The movement had an organ for a few months in the *Ten Hours Advocate*, which was started in September 1846, a weekly paper which makes dull reading when compared with the lively pages of the *League*. But the agitation itself was as polemical as the agitation against the Corn Laws. This was not true of Ashley's part in it. His sense of personal responsibility, his feeling for the dignity of public life, and his dread of exciting popular passion governed his conduct on the platform as everywhere else. Several of his allies were of a different temper, and their rhetoric was as vehement as that of any of the League speakers. The Protectionist papers argued at the time of the Chartist riots that the wildest Chartist orators were less to blame for the violence of class feeling than the orators of the League. Oastler was a match for any of them. When he spoke of teaching children to put needles into the machines they were tending, the *Manchester Guardian* remarked that so reckless a speaker ought to be placed under restraint either by his friends or by the law.

In Parliament there were people like Roebuck who were against all restrictions. There were, at the same time, people like Fielden who were in favour of restricting the hours of adult labour directly and definitely by law. Such men were few. The great majority of members could be divided into two classes. One class would have liked to restrict the hours of persons under eighteen, but preferred to leave such persons unprotected rather than run the risk of injuring industry by restricting the hours of adults. The second class did not want to run the risk of injuring industry by restricting the hours of adults, but preferred to take the risk involved in that reduction, rather than leave children under eighteen working twelve hours a day. The Ten Hours Bill became law in 1847 because in the later stages of the discussions a number of persons like Lord John Russell, Sir George Grey, and Macaulay had passed from the first of these classes to the second.

The great debates in Parliament took place in the years 1844, 1846, and 1847. Peel's Government introduced a Factory Bill in 1844, making a number of detailed improvements in the law. Ashley tried to insert a ten hours' clause in the Government Bill. Opinion was so nicely balanced that Ashley succeeded with one of his amendments by a majority of nine votes, though when the same issue came before the House on a different clause he was defeated by seven votes. Parliament thus threw the Government Bill into confusion. The Government therefore introduced a second Bill, with a plain warning that they would resign if the House of Commons reduced the hours of labour. A great many members who would have liked to support Ashley were not prepared to turn the Government out, and as a consequence of this threat he was beaten when he tried to amend their second Bill, by 297 votes to 159. This year he was supported for the first time by the leading Whigs. The relation of the parties in the house to the parties in the press was curious. The Conservative press in the industrial towns was strongly in favour of the Ten Hours Bill: the Liberal press, with the exception of the *Bradford Observer*, was strongly opposed to it. Peel said that he would resign rather than let the House of Commons pass the Bill which the Conservative press wanted, while leading Liberals, like Lord John Russell, Sir George Grey, and Macaulay, gave strong support to the Bill of which the Liberal press believed, with Peel, that it would be disastrous to industry. The *Leeds Mercury*, the *Universe*, and the *Nonconformist* were angry with Russell and Grey, while the Conservative press was dissatisfied with Peel.

In January 1846 Ashley resigned his seat. He had been converted to Repeal, and he was too conscientious to sit and vote as a Free Trader, having been elected as a Protectionist. Before resigning he introduced a Ten Hours Bill, and this Bill, in Fielden's charge, came up for second reading on May 22, a week after Peel's Bill for the abolition of the Corn Laws had passed its third reading. The Bill was now defeated by ten votes, the opponents (205) consisting of 81 Liberals, 73 Peelites, and 51 Protectionists; the supporters of 71 Liberals, 7 Peelites, and 117 Protectionists. On June 25 Peel's Government fell, and Russell succeeded him as Prime Minister. Conditions were therefore much more favourable, for, though the House of Commons had not changed, the new Prime Minister was a friend and not an opponent. Ashley was still out of the House. Fielden introduced his Bill on January 26, 1847, and its second reading was carried on February 17 by 195 votes to 87. The Whig leaders wanted to make the Bill an Eleven Hours Bill, thinking that the risk of industrial loss would be diminished, and knowing that many mill-owners in the North, like Sir Titus Salt and Marshall of Leeds, had adopted an eleven hours' day. But Peel, though he thought it dangerous to reduce hours at all, preferred ten hours to eleven; for he thought that if Parliament made the smaller change the workmen would continue to agitate for the larger. He and his friends therefore took no part on this issue, and the proposal to substitute eleven for ten was defeated on March 17 by 144 to 66. Russell's Government accepted the decision of the House and gave the Bill the fullest support, overcoming Bright's efforts to kill it by obstruction by promising Government time. In consequence, the Bill became law without difficulty. Brougham and Clarendon attacked the Bill in the Lords, but they were beaten by 53 to 11.

As a result of these two agitations England rang from one end to the other with denunciations of the rich by the rich. Feargus O'Connor or Bronterre O'Brien could not say harsher things than the landlords were saying of the manufacturers and the manufacturers of the landlords. How did a Leaguer describe the life of the agricultural labourer? "What! six shillings a week for wages, and the morning's sun, and the singing of birds, and sportive lambs, and winding streams, and the mountain breeze, and a little wholesome labour—six shillings a week, and all this! And nothing to do with your six shillings a week, but merely to pay your rent, buy your food, clothe yourselves and your families, and lay by something for old age! Happy people!" *Punch*, commenting on the unfortunate remark of the Duke of Norfolk that curry powder was very soothing in an ill-filled stomach, and on discussions that were proceeding about different kinds of diet, suggested that the landlords should hold a competition in peasants instead of in fat cattle. The catalogue might read like this: "No. 1. A short-legged Norfolk labourer. Fed on boiling water and curry powder. Walked thirty miles to the Exhibition. Bred in the Norwich workhouse. First prize." "No. 2. A Hampshire labourer. Supported entirely on starch. Brought in a cab half a mile to the Exhibition by Dr. Buckland, Second prize. . . ." Then what about the mill-worker? On this subject Mr. Ferrand, the member for Bingley, had the sharpest tongue. Indeed, the House of Commons was perpetually engaged in personal controversies of which he was the centre. Here is an account that he gave to the House of Commons of the conditions of life of the textile workpeople. "The poor weavers who are perhaps only receiving 3s. 6d. or 4s. a week, are constantly mulcted in this manner by these overlookers, who have their own wages paid out of what they can deduct from these plundered wretches, and a percentage on the amount. Then again, mark what follows: They have not even the small amount paid in money—it is paid in goods—in rotten corn—in 'cheap flour': and when the poor man carries it home to his wife and

family, after in vain endeavouring to induce his master
to pay him his wages in money, he finds the flour which
he had received as wages in the previous week still
unconsumed, the quality being so bad, that the
stomachs of his sickly children had been unable to
retain it.''

These descriptions were, of course, denounced as
false, but so far as the theme of this chapter is concerned,
whether they were true or false does not matter. They
are cited to show that the worst that could be said of
the rich by the poor was being said by the rich of one
another. Inevitably the strength of class passion was
distracted.

The Chartists might say that if the workman would
listen to them he would obtain blessings in comparison
with which the Repeal of the Corn Laws and the Ten
Hours Bill would seem trifling gains. Some of the
Chartists, following Feargus O'Connor, were even
against Repeal. But when Ebenezer Elliott said that he
was for the Charter but did not want to be starved first,
he spoke for great numbers of working men and women.
In such minds the revolutionary movement was short-
circuited. The battle that Feargus O'Connor was fighting, in which the poor were invited to struggle with the
rich, ceased to be the central spectacle of politics. It
was much more exciting to watch rich men fighting
with rich men, pelting each other with the wrongs of
the poor.

These agitations were important for another reason. A
description has been attempted in an earlier chapter of
the forces and influences that tended to alienate the poor
both from the Established and the Nonconformist
Churches. The Chartist movement scared most of the
religious leaders. These two agitations provided an
opportunity for bringing the Churches into touch with
the feelings and desires of the poor. The Nonconformists
threw themselves into the Repeal movement. At one
League meeting no fewer than 700 Nonconformist clergy

sat on the platform. An issue had arisen, unlike that of
Chartism, on which Nonconformists could take the side
of the poor without disturbing the unity or peace of their
organization. This agitation helped to give Nonconformity its hold on the village labourers. In the final
struggle in the House of Lords, Bishops Thirlwall and
Wilberforce made two of the best speeches on behalf of
Repeal, and the bishops voted for Repeal by 15 to 9,
but in the main the Church had been either neutral or
hostile.

The Nonconformists threw themselves into the Repeal
agitation; the Church took up the Ten Hours Bill. In
the thirties all the Churches were cold to this cause. Bull,
the Bradford parson, speaking at Manchester in April
1833, said that out of 70 clergy in Manchester only two
had come out as public advocates of this reform. "It
cannot be because they are slow to speak, for I have
myself heard the eloquence of your Stowells, your
Newtons, and your McColls." In the forties the *Burnley
Bee,* a newspaper started to oppose the Bill, complained
of the leading part taken by the Church in the agitation.
The Vicars of Leeds, Bradford, Wakefield, Huddersfield, Dewsbury, and of many smaller towns, acted as
chairmen regularly at meetings for the Ten Hours Bill;
another Lancashire Vicar, Canon Wray, took the same
part at Manchester; the Vicar of Leigh prepared a petition at his own expense. The Church paper, the
Guardian, gave strong support to the Bill. "We must
have a time to eat and a time to sleep; a time to rise up
and a time to sit down; 'a time,' as it has been elo-
quently said, 'to live in and a time to die in'; a time to
shape life into immortality:

> Continuo has leges, aeternaque foedera nobis
> Imposuit natura;*

Nature will avenge herself for the robbery if she is de-

* "Such the eternal bond
And such the laws by Nature's hand imposed."
—Virgil, Georgics, I. 60

frauded by oppression and cupidity.'' The Nonconformists were less active. Kydd names in his history a
few Nonconformist ministers, including the famous
William Dawson, and he mentions that one of them, a
Baptist, gave offence to some of the principal members
of his congregation. This is not surprising, for the
strongest opponent of the Bill in the press was the *Leeds
Mercury,* the ablest spokesman of Nonconformist
politics, and the *Nonconformist* also followed John
Bright. ''The Ten Hours Bill, founded upon a vicious
principle, would curtail the rights of labour without
permanently increasing its comforts. It would cost
the poor man too much—it would ultimately repay
him nothing.'' The *Watchman,* the Wesleyan Methodist paper, was neutral, both on the Ten Hours
Bill and the Repeal of the Corn Laws, holding that the
one question of supreme importance was that of ''in-
fusing as much as possible of the old Protestant spirit
—the spirit of our Reformers—into the next Representa-
tive Assembly of our land.'' Thus these two agitations,
by bringing the Nonconformists and the Established
Church into politics on the side of the poor in one or
other of their quarrels with the rich, helped to soften the
impression that the life and circumstances of the
Churches made on the imagination of the working
classes. The Nonconformist clergy befriended the poor
against the landowner; the Church clergy befriended the
poor against the manufacturer.

The life and career of these agitations affected profoundly the class war of the forties. The success that
followed them gave a new tone to working life from the
fifties. The Repeal of the Corn Laws removed a sense of
injustice in a dramatic manner and helped to produce
a great expansion of trade, which eased the hardships
of town life. The passing of the Ten Hours Act was even
more important as an influence on the imagination of the
poor. There were many who said that it was wrong to
make food dearer for the poor, and the Repeal of the

Corn Laws signified the success of that contention.* The passing of the Ten Hours Act signified the success of a contention that had a harder battle to fight: the contention that the workman had a right to a share in the culture and leisure enjoyed by other classes. The Factory agitation, starting as a crusade for the protection of children, had ended as a successful campaign for the right of the working classes to a larger life.

* " The immediate effect of Repeal was to prevent a rise in the price of bread, not to reduce the price. The fall in prices did not come till the seventies."—Venn, *Foundation of Agricultural Economics,* p. 316.

CHAPTER XII

THE BATTLE FOR PUBLIC HEALTH

WHILST the battles for the Abolition of the Corn Laws and for the Ten Hours Bill were going on, another and a less spectacular struggle was taking place. Its object was to improve the conditions of town life, described, in all their squalor, in an earlier chapter. This campaign enjoyed less of what would now be called publicity than the other two, and its success, though considerable, was less decisive. The story of this struggle, carried on by a handful of professional men and politicians, is worth telling. It shows how slow the governing classes were to recognize that, when large masses of men and women are herded together, certain elementary provisions are needed, not only to make life tolerable, but to preserve life itself.

The general arrangement of English local government to-day follows certain definite principles. Over every area there is some local responsible authority with duties imposed and powers bestowed by Parliament. These authorities are grouped in a hierarchy from the Parish meeting to the County Council, the powers exercised by a county borough differing from those exercised by a non-county borough, and the duties of an urban district council differing from those of a rural district council. Above this system of local authorities we find some central department such as the Ministry of Health or that of Education, with certain limited powers of inspection and control. The local and central authorities are connected also in another manner, for the local authorities subject to this kind of pressure are stimulated by direct help from the central government in the form of grants in aid. English local government differs from American local government in giving more power to the central authorities, whilst it differs from local government on the Continent in giving greater freedom to the local authority.

When statesmen and thinkers set out to attack the evils described in an earlier chapter, scarcely any of this machinery existed. There was no Local Government Board or Ministry of Health. In the towns there were no local authorities with effective powers, and in the country there were rarely authorities with any powers at all. Grants in aid of local services were unknown. The old muddled system of government by Corporations, or Manor Courts, or Improvement Commissioners, with all its abuses, had been swept away by the Municipal Corporations Reform Act of 1835, and Town Councils, elected by ratepayers, had taken its place; but very few of these Councils had full powers of draining, cleansing, and paving.

The campaign began in 1838. Edwin Chadwick, the man who took the first step, may be regarded as the chief benefactor of his age if you look at the power and courage with which he brought abuses to light, and as its evil genius if you dwell on the fate of any plan of reform that fell into his hands. This unpopular man used in this case for his purpose an unpopular institution. In 1838 the Poor Law Commission published a report calling attention to the vast burden thrown on the rates by sickness and epidemics, the result of sanitary conditions. The report contained some striking evidence about Whitechapel and Bethnal Green, given by three doctors, all of them famous either then or later—Southwood Smith, Arnott, and Kay. Chadwick suggested privately to Bishop Blomfield that he should ask in the House of Lords for a similar return for the whole of England. The request was granted. Chadwick set to work, and in 1842 the Poor Law Commission published his justly celebrated Report on the Sanitary Condition of the Labouring Population of Great Britain.

When Blomfield moved in the Lords, R. A. Slaney, one of the most useful and active of members, moved in the House of Commons, proposing the appointment of a Select Committee. This Committee, known as the Health of Towns Committee, reported in June 1840. It recommended a general Building Act, a general Sewage Act, and the creation of a Board of Health in every town, with instructions to look after the water-supply, burial grounds, open spaces, lodging-houses, and slums. Southwood Smith, who like Chadwick had been Bentham's private secretary, gave evidence before this Committee, and took steps to interest the new Home Secretary, Lord Normanby, in the cause of sanitary reform. A visit to the slums of East London made Normanby as ardent for reform as Southwood Smith himself, and he promptly introduced two Bills in the House of Lords (January 29, 1841)—one for the regulation of buildings, and the other for the regulation of drainage—of a drastic and revolutionary character. The second Bill was split up in committee into two Bills, the Drainage of Buildings Bill and the Borough Improvement Bill. These three Bills gave town councils the power to take land compulsorily, with an appeal to the Department of Woods and Forests, and provided for the appointment of surveyors and assistant surveyors by town councils and J.P.s. The surveyor had to be notified before a building was begun. Houses were not to be built back to back, or below the level of the ground if without an area; no cellar was to be used as a dwelling without a window and fireplace and open area; houses were not to be built in close alleys, and streets were to be 30 feet wide when there was a carriage-way, and 20 feet wide in other cases. No house was to be built until the site was drained, and drains were to be constructed for houses already built. New streets were to be levelled under the direction of the Commissioners of Sewers.

There was little reported debate in the House of Lords. One member proposed to exclude Birmingham, but for the most part the Bills received strong support. The Mayor and Burgesses of Leeds sent a petition in favour of the Drainage Bill.

The Bills passed the Lords, but in May the Whig Government fell, and in the Election that followed they were defeated. Melbourne was succeeded by Peel as Prime Minister, a change for the better; Normanby was succeeded by Sir James Graham as Home Secretary, a change for the worse.

Next year Normanby introduced his Bills again in the Lords (February 7, 1842), this time as a private member. The Bills went to a Select Committee which took evidence from London, Manchester, Liverpool, and Leeds. As a result of this evidence the important clause forbidding back-to-back houses disappeared.

This particular clause was supported by one witness only, a London engineer. The Liverpool witness said that the Liverpool town council had considered the proposal and rejected it on the ground of expense. The Manchester witnesses said that the clause would raise the cost of the cheapest house from £96 to £119, and the third-class house, generally occupied by skilled artisans, from £141 to £179. The labouring classes lived in the main in back-to-back houses, covering 16 superficial yards, for which they paid a rent of 2s. to 3s., the landlord paying all the rates and making repairs inside and out. Working men with large families took the double house, being enabled to pay the rent by the earnings of their children and the rent they received from lodgers. The Town Clerk of Leeds was also opposed to the clause, contending that it would drive the working class into lodgings, but he held that it should be made compulsory to provide an open space of 30 or 40 square yards at the end of every four or five cottages. House property was the favourite investment of small men in Leeds, and there were 1,200 freeholders who had bought houses out of their savings. This evidence was too much for the Committee, and the proposal was abandoned.*

Normanby's Bills were reported to the House of Commons but they were postponed in return for the promise of a Government Bill in the following year. Peel's Government decided, however, in 1843, not to introduce a Bill but to set up a Commission on the Health of Towns. This Commission, of which the Duke of Buccleuch was Chairman, contained among its members two active members of Parliament, R. A. Slaney and Lord Lincoln, and two distinguished men of science, Lyon Playfair and H. T. De la Beche. The Commission issued its first Report in the summer of 1844, and its second in the spring of 1845. The education of public

* Two years after Normanby's Committee had been warned by the Chairman of the Sewerage and Paving Committee of the Manchester Commissioners of Police that the cost was prohibitive, this reform was effected by a local Act, for Heron, the Town Clerk of Manchester, told the Sanitary Commission in 1869 that a local Act of 1844, requiring that every house should have a privy and ash-pit behind it, had put an end to the building of back-to-back houses. "The consequence of that legislation has been that in Manchester, since 1844, the building of back-to-back houses, which is one of the most crying nuisances that can be imagined, has been illegal." In Bradford an attempt to bring about this reform by a similar method made in the early sixties was defeated by the speculative builders (see 1869 Sanitary Commission Report, p. 122, and Cudworth, *Historical Notes of Corporation of Bradford*, p. 145). Mr. J. B. Priestley has given a description of the Bradford back-to-back houses in *The Good Companions*: "the product of an ingenious architectural scheme that crammed four dwelling-houses into the space of two and enabled some past citizens to drive a carriage and pair and take their wives and daughters to the Paris Exhibition in 1867." The proposal to forbid the building of these houses by a general law was revived by Sir Benjamin Hall when President of the Board of Health in 1855. Hall said that he had received communications on the subject from Sunderland, Leicester, Coventry, and other places, and that some of the largest towns in the kingdom were in favour of this reform (House of Commons, January 23, 1855). But nothing came of the proposal, and these houses were not made illegal until 1909.

opinion thus continued, and the local legislation of the next few years shows that the new ideas were making progress outside Parliament. Birkenhead, Nottingham, and Liverpool all took action in the spirit of Normanby's proposals. The Birkenhead Improvement Commissioners obtained an Act in 1843, which set aside a large area for a park for public recreation, forbade the building of houses in close courts, regulated the size of rooms and the number of windows, compelled owners of houses to supply privies, and provided that streets should be 24 feet wide where there was a carriage-way, and 12 where there was not.

At Nottingham an Inclosure Act of 1845, enclosing 1,069 acres, set apart 130 for recreation, and laid down strict rules for the development of the rest of the area. The streets were to be 36 feet wide, alleys and courts 20 feet, and buildings were not to be higher than the width of the streets. Each house was to have a separate privy, and a yard or garden thirty feet long. No dwelling-house was to adjoin another building on more than two sides; no room without a fireplace or proper ventilation was to be used as a workshop or bedroom; every house was to have three bedrooms of certain fixed dimensions. Cesspools were never to be within ten feet of a house. Liverpool, having obtained an Act in 1842, proceeded to amend it by a much more drastic Act in 1846. This Act made regulations about houses, courts, and cellars; provided for "effectually sewering and draining the borough," laid it down that no cellars under any house in a court were to be let as dwellings, that no houses were to be erected without drains, and that every new street should be at least 30 feet wide. An interesting feature of this Act was the clause providing for the appointment of a duly qualified medical practitioner as Medical Officer of Health. The first doctor to hold the office was W. H. Duncan, Physician to the Liverpool Infirmary, who had already laid the foundations of his fame as a sanitary reformer and a great public servant.

In 1844 the Health of Towns Commission published its first Report. This Report was largely the work of Chadwick. Fifty large towns had been surveyed. In 42 the drainage, and in 31 the water-supply, were decidedly bad; there were only six in which the water-supply was good, and scarcely one in which the drainage was good. Next year the Commissioners made their recommendations. It was essential, they argued, that the responsibility now divided between different local bodies for paving, draining, cleansing the streets, and supplying water should be concentrated in the hands of a single authority; that those authorities should have additional powers, and their districts be made co-extensive with the natural areas for drainage. But their most novel suggestion was the proposal that the Crown should have power to inspect and supervise the work of the local authorities. *The Times* had attacked Normanby's Bill in February 1841 as "the reckless and wanton invasion of property and liberty," but in May of that year Delane became editor, and from this time onwards it was a powerful and steadfast friend to the cause of public health. It gave a warm support to the report of the Commissioners, and a general support to the Bill based on its Report introduced by Lord Lincoln in 1845. Lincoln explained that the Government did not propose to proceed with the Bill that year, but had introduced it to give the opportunity for discussion in the recess.

Lincoln's Bill made the Home Office the central department, and gave the Home Secretary power to appoint inspectors whose duty it would be to hold local inquiries and prepare plans for boundaries mapping out England into districts. Local authorities were to be elected for these areas by ratepayers with a property qualification, but in corporate towns a certain number of Commissioners were to be elected from the town council, and a certain number from the borough magistrates. The Bill excited some opposition from the local authorities. It received a general but discriminating support from the Health of Towns Association, an educational and propagandist body formed by Southwood Smith, of which Normanby, Ashley, Tooke, and Joseph Toynbee were active members. Next year politics were thrown into confusion by the crisis over the Repeal of the Corn Laws. The Conservative Party was broken up; Peel resigned in June 1846, and Lincoln's Bill made no further progress. Parliament, however, passed two useful measures: one, the Baths and Wash-houses Act, which authorized borough councils to establish baths and wash-houses out of the rates; the other the Nuisance Removal Act. The second was passed as a temporary Act, but it was afterwards made permanent.

On Peel's fall, Lord John Russell became Prime Minister for the first time. Events had thus brought back the Whigs to power, and though Normanby had left politics to become Ambassador in Paris, it was known that sanitary reform would be one of their principal measures. The *Leeds Intelligencer* published an enthusiastic article on the prospects of reform. "This species of legislation on so vast and comprehensive a scale is novel and as grand as it is novel. We know of nothing which so much marks the kind of enlightened relations that are springing up in society as this interference by the State on behalf of the health and physical well-being of our industrial classes. Hitherto public cleanliness in our great towns and cities has been an aristocratic appendage and an elegant luxury. The legislation announced last session, and about to be executed in this, has laid down the principle that the health, cleanliness, and purity of the poor man's street and dwelling just as much as the rich man's are to be a primary concern of the State. This is true democracy. Let restless, shallow-headed Brights chatter as they will about democratic reforms."

Unhappily these hopes were in part disappointed, for the Reform movement took at one point a wrong turn, and the cause of public health suffered in consequence.

It is not surprising that a study of the conditions revealed in the Reports of the Health of Towns Commission had impressed politicians with the negligence of the
local authorities. The government of the towns was
largely in the hands of men with limited horizons: men
chiefly concerned for economy and uninspired by large
or generous ambitions. This class predominated among
electors and elected. In some cases the obstacles to
reform were even more serious, for it happened sometimes that the men who were put in charge of the health
of the town were themselves interested in the maintenance of abuses. But Parliament was itself a good deal to
blame. The Municipal Corporations Act of 1835 was an
unimaginative measure little calculated to fire ambition
or public spirit, and withholding power that the local
authorities needed for effective action. It was clearly
desirable, therefore, that the statesman who wished to
introduce some measure of control or guidance from the
centre should avoid any unnecessary collision with local
sentiment.

Lord Lincoln had proposed, in his 1845 Bill, that the
Home Office should act as a central department. The
Health of Towns Association had objected, in an unfortunate moment, that the Home Office had a great deal
on its hands already, and that this new task needed a
new authority. In this suggestion there lurked a danger.
For sanitary reformers were tempted to look for a precedent to the Poor Law Commission. In that case, they
reflected, a special body exercising special powers had
rescued a nation from scandals that had grown up under
the lax administration of local authorities. The old Poor
Law authorities had been negligent, incompetent, and
sometimes corrupt: they had been put on one side by a
board of energetic men armed by Parliament with exceptional means of interference. The sanitary authorities where
they existed were negligent, incompetent, and sometimes
corrupt. Why should not the same remedy be applied?
Lord Morpeth, the Commissioner of Woods and Forests

in the Government, the Minister in charge of this reform, accepted this suggestion and he proposed to set up a Board resembling the Poor Law Commission in its structure and also in its relation to Parliament. This Board was not to be an ordinary Department under the care and orders of a Minister responsible to Parliament, but a body of Commissioners, of equal authority, with a Minister sitting at the table as an ordinary member.

In the Bill as introduced on March 30, 1847, this body was given large powers both of initiating and superintending sanitary reform. It could hold a local inquiry, define a district, and set up a public health authority for that district. The boundaries of a town could be extended if necessary. In the corporate towns the town council would act as the local authority: in non-corporate towns local Commissioners would be appointed, partly by the Crown and partly by the ratepayers. These local bodies would appoint local surveyors and inspectors of nuisances: they would look after the streets, drainage, building regulations, nuisances like those of smoke, slaughter-houses, and cemeteries: they would have the power to construct waterworks and gasworks. For the expenses of permanent works they would have power to borrow money and recover the principal and interest by moderate instalments, not from the owners but from the occupiers. "In this manner we hope we shall remove what we consider to be the chief obstacle to improvements in towns, which is the opposition of owners to what they consider the serious expense attending them." The Board was to have a general superintending power.

Lincoln criticized the scheme on the ground that it gave too much power to the central authority, and that town councils, being political in character, could not safely be given control over surrounding areas. Hume and Brotherton were favourable, but Morpeth soon found that he could not hope to hold his own against all the powerful interests that were threatened, or thought themselves to be threatened, by his Bill. The land-

owners, whose opposition he had hoped to disarm,
resisted his Bill from first to last.* Their spokesman
complained that landowners in the neighbourhood might
have to pay for draining a town. Morpeth said that the
landowners were not affected. Brotherton administered
a sharp rebuke. "Hon. members connected with those
districts were very sensitive; but he could tell them that
in the suburbs of large towns, landowners had derived
great advantages from the industry of their neighbours,
and he knew cases where landowners had their income
advanced from £5,000 to £20,000 a year, without doing
a single thing to promote the welfare of the inhabitants
by whom they were so much benefited." The various
vested interests, water companies, gas companies, burial
companies, and others, offered so effective a resistance
that many of the clauses relating to these subjects were
completely remodelled. The more general fears of
property and business found an appropriate representa-
tive in Hudson, the railway king, member of Parliament
for Sunderland, and Lord Mayor of York. More than
once he drew upon himself the fire of *The Times*. "The
Honourable Member for Sunderland, to do him justice,
is a perfectly consistent legislator. From one simple
rule he has never deviated since the day when his
splendid promises prevailed with the electors of that
borough. He denounces everything whatever except railways . . . railways are both medicine and meat. . . . In
the present increase of private speculation, conducted, of
course, on the most private principles, it becomes the

* *The Times* called the Bill "the object of singular Protectionist aversion."—July 3, 1847. Dickens composed a
petition for such objectors. "The taxation for the purpose of
draining and ameliorating such would fall most unjustly and
oppressively on your memorialists, whose manor house, lawns,
pleasure grounds, arable lands, and pasture grounds could
neither directly nor indirectly derive any benefit whatever
from the purpose for which hereditaments and tenements
would be rated in pursuance of the powers of the Public
Health Act."—Crotch, *Charles Dickens as Social Reformer*,
p. 103.

more necessary for the State to provide that the interests of the public shall not be thrust into a corner. Railways are made to pay, and Mr. Hudson himself understands how to carry out that principle with the most offensive rigour." Morpeth hoped at first to save his Bill by making large concessions. He began by dropping London. He limited the Bill to corporate towns, allowing non-corporate towns to come under the Act on petition; he agreed that all local Commissioners should be elected by the ratepayers and none by the Crown; he took the sting, and, as some critics said, the virtue, out of the clauses about gas and water. Yet he had in the summer to abandon his Bill. But the year was not wasted, for several Acts were passed, consolidating clauses generally found in local Improvements Bills, in order to cheapen and simplify local legislation. A town authority, wishing to obtain powers for providing gas, water, and other improvements, could incorporate all or any of these clauses in its own Act, thereby saving itself trouble and expense.

Morpeth returned to his task early in the following year, introducing his new Bill on February 10, 1848. The Bill differed in some respects from its predecessor, but the creation of a central board on the model of the Poor Law Commission was the most important feature of the new Bill as it had been of the old. London was excluded. Local boards were to compel owners or occupiers to provide house drains, to see that there was a sufficient supply of water, and to appoint a surveyor and inspector of nuisances. Other duties were permissive. The local authority might make by-laws about the removal of filth: they might alter sewers, pave streets, provide places for public recreation, and appoint an officer of health. "If this Bill will not do," said *The Times*, "what will? . . . Unless objectors are prepared with some positive measures of their own, we really think they had better hold their peace and have done with it." The objectors were not disposed to follow this advice.

The feature of the Bill which provoked the most general criticism was the proposal to establish a central authority with the power both of initiating and superintending reform. This was represented as a French principle foreign to English tradition and obnoxious to English sentiment. These objections were pressed in Parliament by a member who was under no suspicion of speaking for any vested interest, Urquhart, an interesting and romantic figure in the politics of the time, and they were pressed outside Parliament by the historian Toulmin Smith. *The Times* replied to these arguments that centralization and government patronage were evils, but that in this case the alternatives were worse. "A town of manufacturers and speculators is apt to leave the poor to shift for themselves, to stew in cellars and garrets, nor are landlords and farmers apt to care much for cottages. . . . Something of a central authority is necessary to wrestle with the selfishness of wealth."

But whatever the virtues or defects of central authorities, it is clear that the particular form of centralization adopted, the setting up of a central board composed on the provocative model of the Poor Law Commission, was a lamentable blunder. It roused the determined opposition of town councils. The Bill did not spare their dignity, and it brought their delegates to London in hot haste to denounce it as intolerable tyranny. The hostility to the Bill found its most uncompromising expression in the *Leeds Mercury,* which went so far as to withdraw its support from Lord Morpeth when he appeared as a candidate for the West Riding in the autumn of the year. "What populous and enlightened towns," it wrote, "like Bradford, Halifax, Huddersfield, Wakefield, and a score of others in the manufacturing district round us want, is simple and efficient means for attending to their own sanitary regulation." In the same article the editor referred to Leeds as "this borough in which so much has been done and projected for the public health." Nor was the *Leeds Mercury* concerned only for the rights and dignities of the large towns. "We disapprove of opposition on behalf of existing corporate towns only: it would abandon every non-corporate place to the mercy of the framers of the Bill."

But even the opposition of the town councils to the Bill revealed the existence of a local demand for some sort of reform. A great deal had been done by the propaganda of bodies like the Health of Towns Association, by the pressure of parsons and doctors, and in some towns by working-class associations, to create alarm and indignation about the state of the towns. Hence even the town councils, whether from conviction or fear, did not adopt a purely destructive tone. The Bradford town council, for example, rejected a proposal to send an angry petition merely condemning the Bill, adopting instead a petition which, whilst hostile to the scheme of the Bill, admitted the need for strong measures. The Mayor of Leeds published an alternative scheme which would have given a central board certain limited powers of inspection. The Mayor of Bolton, while denouncing the Government proposals, proceeded to obtain and to publish a detailed report on the condition of Bolton from the Secretary of the Mechanics' Institute, which was full of the most dreadful revelations. All these authorities, in fact, though thrown into violent opposition by Morpeth's proposal, recognized the necessity for action.

The strength of the demand for reform is shown also by a study of the local press. In each of the protesting towns important local papers defended the Bill, some in its most drastic form, some urging certain modifications. Thus the *Manchester Guardian*, while agreeing with the Manchester town council that the new authority was given too detailed a control, held strongly that some control was needed. The spokesman of the Manchester town council had argued that the new Bill did nothing for Manchester that was not already done under the Manchester Improvement Act. The *Manchester Guardian* commented dryly that "in practice the effect would be

the making of private drains the general rule, not as now
the rather rare exception." The news columns of the
paper gave, indeed, ample justification for the tone of
the leading articles. On September 13, the Public
Accountant reported that nearly one-third of the ash-
pits in the borough were in a condition dangerous to
health in consequence of a reduction of the scavenging
force. A few weeks later, the chairman of one of the
committees of the town council explained that he was
going to save the rates £4,000 a year by reverting to the
old practice of hand-sweeping in the streets, though, as
the *Manchester Guardian* pointed out, the condition of
the Manchester streets when that method was in force
had been notorious. The *Birmingham Journal* too, in
spite of the opposition of the town council, gave the
strongest support to the Bill, arguing that the expense
of all the necessary sanitary provision for the poorer
classes would be defrayed by a rate not exceeding 4*d*.
per week per house, but that unless the superintending
power of the central authority was preserved, the Bill
would be inoperative. The *Leeds Intelligencer* was so
much impressed by the filth and squalor of the streets of
Leeds, that it welcomed the proposal to give a central
body far-reaching powers. The *Bradford Observer*,
though supporting the petition of the town council, made
it clear that it would prefer the Bill with its imperfections
to no Bill at all, and when the opponents of the Bill
were hopeful of defeating it, the *Observer* rallied to its
defence, pointing to the Bradford death-rate. The
average age of death at Pateley Bridge was 36, and at
Bradford it was 20, but the middle classes lived as long
in Bradford as in Pateley Bridge. It was the Bradford
poor who made this startling difference. The defeat of
the Bill would mean "that the poor victims of our dirty
lanes and false patriotism would be left to fester and
die." The *Bolton Chronicle*, too, published a whole
series of articles on the revelations of the report on the
state of the town: "For abundant dirt, for lack of

drainage, for crowded and disgusting homes, for the numbers sweltering amidst noxious airs and poisonous gases, for pestilential nuisances, for defective sewerage and complete absence of all sanitary arrangements, properly so called, we can justly claim, if we do not bear away, the palm. There may be other towns as bad in these respects, but can anybody point us out a worse?''

Morpeth's Bill, then, in its early form, though it provoked organized opposition from town councils, received a considerable amount of local support. Several representatives of local authorities met in London to put their objections to the Bill, and as a result of negotiations Morpeth allowed the Town Clerk of Manchester, together with Brotherton and Beckett, M.P. for Leeds, to confer with the draughtsmen of the Bill to help to remodel it. In this process the general superintending power of the new department disappeared. Lord Lincoln, who had criticized the Bill as giving too great a control to the central authority, argued justly that this surrender went too far in the other direction. Even after these concessions had been made, the Bill struggled with great difficulty on to the Statute Book. Disraeli said that it owed its success to Morpeth's great personal popularity.

The Public Health Act of 1848 set up for five years a Central Board of Health, consisting of three members, one of them ex-officio the Commissioner of Woods and Forests. It provided also for the creation of local Boards of Health, who were to be endowed with certain powers and charged with certain duties. In a municipal borough the Board of Health was to be the town council, elsewhere it was to be a special Board elected by the ratepayers on the same plan as the Board of Guardians. A town council might adopt the Act, in which case it could exercise these powers without the expense of a special local Act. But the Central Board, in certain circumstances, might take action in places where the Act was not adopted. If the death-rate in any place exceeded 23 per 1,000, or if 10 per cent of the inhabitants asked for

it, the Central Board might hold an inquiry and create
a local Board of Health district and a local Board of
Health. In such a case the Act might be forced on a
local authority that did not want it. A town council
might be converted into a Board of Health against
its will.

An Act which gave just so much power and no more
was ill-contrived for its purpose, and it was made worse
by the choice of the Board to execute it. It is difficult to
understand how Ministers, painfully aware as they must
have been of the atmosphere of resentment and suspicion in which the Act was received, came to choose the
most hated man in England as a member of the Board.
For Chadwick, who would have been excellent if you
wanted to make a popular law odious, was expected in
this case to make an obnoxious law attractive. Whatever chance the Act had of success was thrown away,
when the Government announced that the new Board
would consist of Lord Morpeth, Lord Ashley, and Edwin
Chadwick.

The defects of the Act became very plain during the
lifetime of the Board. The Act enabled the Board to
force the hand of a reluctant local authority, but not to
compel that authority to take any effective action. It
was indeed less likely rather than more likely that a
sullen authority would carry out a measure thrust upon
it. The Central Board had no power of superintendence
or inspection, and the local authority was in no mood to
take guidance from an authority whose powers it
resented. If a local authority chose to neglect its duty
it could defy the Board of Health. The extreme case was
that of Newcastle. An outbreak of cholera in Newcastle
led the Government to send a Commission of Enquiry in
January 1854. This Commission reported that the filthy
condition of that town (of which Palmerston once said
that the account of it made a civilized man shudder)
was due to nuisances which the Corporation had the
power but not the will to suppress, and that there were

some members of the town council to whom these nuisances were a source of profit. The Board of Health was powerless.

The defects of the Board were also apparent. After making an admirable report on the water-supply and the burial arrangements of London, both of them in a scandalous condition, they proceeded to recommend that the duty and power of burying the dead and providing drainage and water for the metropolis should be assigned to the central authority. A Bill designed on this extraordinary basis was passed in 1850, but it was of course unworkable, and it was repealed in 1852. *The Times*, reviewing this ambitious scheme when the Board fell, reminded Chadwick that the Jupiter of antiquity had been a modest person, for he had been content with the sky, leaving the sea to Neptune and the infernal regions to Pluto. Such proposals justified the suspicion with which local authorities had watched the creation of this Board. Its reports proved the necessity for reforms, but its proposals embarrassed their execution.

The Board lasted six years, and, as has been seen, it made many of the mistakes to be expected from Chadwick's want of judgment and want of tact. But its career marks an important stage in the history of public health. The Act was adopted in some 200 places. A separate local Act would have cost each of these places about £2,000. These places included several of the growing industrial towns where sanitary measures were specially needed, such as Bolton, Bradford, Hartlepool, Merthyr Tydfil, Preston, Sunderland, Wakefield, Wigan, and Wolverhampton. The Report of the Board reviewing its career showed that at Preston, Lancaster, Wigan, and other places the Board had given help and expert advice about water and drainage, and that it had sanctioned applications to mortgage the rates for improvements for sums amounting altogether to over a million. Incidentally, also, the Act was the cause of improvements in towns where it was not adopted, for

Leeds and Birmingham and other large towns, wishing to keep out the Board, promoted Bills of their own. Birmingham spent £10,000 in this way rather than accept the general Act. Newcastle also adopted an Act, but treated its own Act with as little respect as if it had been Chadwick's.

The Board also deserved credit for two Housing Acts passed in 1851, one of them described by Dickens as the best measure ever passed in Parliament. This Act made compulsory the licensing and inspection of all common lodging-houses. The other Act, which empowered local authorities to raise a rate and build lodging-houses, was a dead letter from the first. Shaftesbury, formerly Ashley, was in charge of these Bills. He also brought before the House of Lords the hardships and overcrowding caused by improvement and railway schemes. A Committee was appointed at his instance, but nothing came of its recommendations.

The Board lasted till 1854, when the House of Commons got rid of it. The Government tried to save the Board by dropping Chadwick and putting the Board under the Home Office. These concessions did not avail, and the Board was extinguished by 74 votes to 65. The place of this anomalous department was taken by a Board of Ministers with a paid president. This new department retained until 1858 the powers vested in the old Board, but it was now in the hands of Sir Benjamin Hall, a reformer but a keen critic of Chadwick, who was under no suspicion of wishing to limit or discourage local autonomy. Hall put an end to a bad method of employing his staff, which had added to the unpopularity of his predecessors. He made the engineers employed by the department its full-time servants, removed altogether from private practice.

The long struggle to make her town life healthy and decent, in which England has been engaged ever since the Industrial Revolution, took a definite character at this time. The Improvement Commissioners set up by

eighteenth-century practice had tried to make town life
healthy and decent for the richer classes. In the thirties
Chadwick inaugurated a new and more ambitious
effort, the effort to make town life healthy and tolerable
for all classes. However unhappy his plans, he deserves
the utmost credit for that bold initiative.

We can see to-day that of all the tasks set to the
English people at that time none was more pressing
than this. Unfortunately, other tasks and other interests
attracted the main strength of the wealth, the statesmanship, and the energy of the nation. For England was as
mad about railways in the forties as she had been, in
Boulton's phrase, about steam mills in the twenties.
When few of her towns had sewers or water, paved or
lighted streets, Railway Bills were passed through
Parliament authorizing the raising of over £300,000,000.
The Times, which fought a gallant battle against this
waste of power, remarked that Macaulay's New
Zealander would find that England had brought herself
to the verge of bankruptcy by building viaducts at a
moment when 300 streets in a rich district of the metropolis were without a sewer. Bradford, with 100,000
people, started to attack her disgraceful squalor by
spending something like £3,000 a year. Property owners
still preferred dirt to expenditure. *The Times* warned
these economists that they would lose in the end: "The
rates paid by the rich are regulated by the sickness to
which they abandon the poor. Twenty pounds expended
in the sewerage of a blind alley would save fifty pounds
to be otherwise raised by the overseers of the poor."
There were moments when the scare of cholera brought
this argument home, but in normal times it made little
impression. The scale of values represented by the large
investment in railways and the reluctance to spend anything on the English town, meant that the average rich
man believed in the remedy of the Industrial Revolution,
and held that if enterprise were encouraged, this new town
population could be safely left to itself. As late as 1848,

it was argued in the House of Commons that property
was in danger from the proposal to allow a town council
to make a park.

The politics of the age reflected this atmosphere. Mr.
Temperley has said that as you watch Gladstone making
up the nation's accounts as neatly as a grocer, you can
see the spirit of the age fashioning greatness in its pattern. This age produced half a dozen of the most eloquent
and the most persuasive speakers that have ever engaged
in English politics. Nobody who studied the master-
pieces of this art, whether he turned to Palmerston or
Cobden, to Peel or Bright, to Gladstone or Disraeli,
would have any idea of the battle that was raging at this
time between health and disease, between life and death,
in the English towns. Other questions filled the minds of
the great orators who could make what seemed important to themselves seem important to the nation.
A public man, conscious of power and principle, setting
out on a career in politics, would dream in the flights of
his ambition of the office of Chancellor of the Exchequer, or Secretary of State for Foreign Affairs; the
offices concerned with the English towns were regarded
as the lesser duties of Government, departments which a
man would enter by one door and leave by another for
some more attractive or distinguished appointment. "It
is of course, to be expected," said *The Times*, "that the
tenacious spirit of 'protection' would fight every inch of
ground and surrender no vested interest even in the
foulest filth without a struggle. But we are not to be persuaded that stench and smoke could have preserved that
which corn and sugar lost, if they had but been attacked
with half the same determination." The attack on dirt,
disease, and death was carried on in an atmosphere in
which men were thinking all the time of other things.
Governments with the Health of Towns Reports before
them never dreamed of making grants for public health.
The utmost they would do was to lend money at 5 per
cent, repayable first in 30 and then in 20 years.

Two orators at different times did for the English towns what Peel and Cobden did for free trade. One was cholera, the other was the cotton famine. The Town Improvements of the forties followed the cholera scare: in the sixties the Government met the distress into which the cotton famine threw Lancashire by granting loans for Public Works at $3\frac{1}{2}$ per cent, under two Acts passed in 1862 and 1863, and Villiers, the President of the Poor Law Board, issued an admirable circular, calling attention to the great need for improvements in the Lancashire towns, the want of sewers and drains, of parks and gardens, and of good supplies of water. In two years nearly £2,000,000 was spent on these purposes.

Pushing gallantly against great difficulties, a few men like Chadwick, Slaney, Bishop Blomfield, Normanby, Lincoln, Ashley, Morpeth, Toynbee, and Hume, with the powerful help of Delane and Dickens, taught the nation, however slowly, the lesson of the Chartist agitation. The Acts that they put on the Statute Book between 1845 and 1854 showed that Parliament had become aware of a problem to which the statesmen of the thirties had been blind. In the thirties the English town was a raw settlement, where men and women lived as men and women live on a gold-field. Twenty years later some of these towns were busy paving and draining their neglected streets, and a few of them were building libraries and making public parks.

CHAPTER XIII

THE NEW SPIRIT

IF English life had kept its bleak and unsympathetic character unchanged, the distractions that drew off the strength of the class conflict of the thirties would not have had more than a temporary effect. But after the forties there was a slow and gradual improvement in the conditions and temper of social life. This was due partly to economic causes. The Repeal of the Corn Laws was followed by a period of growing prosperity. Further, as Professor Cole has pointed out in the *Short History of the Working Class Movement*, industry had suffered up to nearly the middle of the century from a shortage of available capital. The position of the employer was eased, and his risks lessened in this respect by the Bank Charter Act of 1844 and the Limited Liability Acts of 1855 and 1862. These conditions undoubtedly made it easier for the great educating forces that were released and inspired by the Chartist movement to bring amenities into social life, and so to modify the sharp separation of classes that distinguished the England of the thirties. The Chartists, wishing to strike at the monstrous inequalities of the age, had pressed for the suffrage, because they thought that the provision of political rights would do for the working classes what it had done for the middle classes. They failed, but the instinct for creating a society out of this chaos was prompting other movements which gained power and emphasis from their agitation. Some of these movements were primarily within the working-class world; others were movements in which all classes co-operated. Between them they lifted the English town out of its first barbarism.

We get a vivid idea of the importance and meaning of

the new movements, if we note that the place of the great civic or religious pageants of the past was taken by a new form of festival. Holidays were rare, but Whit-Monday, at least, was kept as a day of rejoicing. Thus, to take a typical Lancashire town, at Blackburn on Whit-Monday, 1884, no less than sixteen Friendly Societies marched in a procession through the town, and the *Blackburn Standard* remarks that though 4,000 persons took part, only one person was taken to the police station at the end of the day.

These societies covered a number of needs and interests. They were mainly sick and burial clubs, but, like the old Roman sick and burial clubs, they provided a form of social life, a world in which poor men and women had common affairs to administer, and common recreations to enjoy. Such societies were, of course, not new, for they were common in some form from about 1740, and Rose had passed an Act in 1793 for their encouragement. Some of these societies were merely collecting societies, for helping thrift and insurance, in which the members took no part, but the large Orders supplied other social needs. They provided the dull life of Lancashire with some colour and pageant. They were blamed by critics for pursuing social entertainment, when they should have been concentrating on thrift, but this was an essential part of their life and function. They set up a society in which the poor man could exercise and develop his taste for fellowship. Men whose lives were spent under the discipline of the mill felt all the need for such an institution especially strongly. Professor Clapham thinks it is not unlikely that no less than two-thirds of the men of Lancashire belonged to some Friendly Society in 1847.

The dignity of each member of a society depends on the observance throughout that society of a recognized standard of behaviour. In the Friendly Society all ruled, and all obeyed; the most important of all forms of equality, equality of manners and bearing, was jealously guarded. Hence the importance that was attached to ritual and ceremonies at lodge meetings. The regulations of the Independent Order of Oddfellows imposed fines for such offences as eating, or reading newspapers or books in the lodge room, for swearing, or singing an indecent song, for leaving the room when a brother was singing, or for neglecting to address the Chair. An elaborate code of manners was thus practised, and membership of a lodge represented a basis and habit of self-respect. The Laws and Regulations of the Oddfellows were published with a preface setting out the "nature and advantages of Odd Fellowship." The Lodge is described as "a useful school of morality, where from various humours, tempers, customs, and circumstances in life, a considerable portion of useful knowledge may be acquired, relative to men and things; where talent of every description may emerge from the clouds of obscurity, and expand itself by a proper exertion, where bashfulness and diffidence may gradually wear off, and a modesty of assurance succeed; where good manners and politeness may be copied from good examples and improved by practice."

Though the workmen had no votes for Parliament and rarely had votes for Town Council or Board of Guardians, there must have been great numbers of working men taking part in the management of Trade Unions, Co-operative Societies, Temperance Societies, and Friendly Societies by the middle of the century. In this way scope was found for instincts and sympathies for which their occupations gave no opportunity. Men were taking decisions, assuming responsibilities, meeting and considering different points of view, expressing and developing their own ideas and sharing in significant ritual and ceremony. Meanwhile the governing world was relaxing the rigours and softening the distinctions of the first industrial age. The change is seen in the mitigation of the Poor Law; a process of which Dickens observed that it showed that no society could enforce the

strict logic of 1834. "I am convinced that its philosophers would sink any Government, any cause, any
doctrine, even the most righteous. There is a sense and
humanity in the mass in the long run that will not
bear them; and they will wreck their friends always,
as they wrecked them in the working of the Poor
Law Bill."

The change is seen also in the religious life of the
time. "There is no Church, and never was one," said
Landor, "in which the Ministers of religion have so little
intercourse with the people as the English. Sunday is the
only day that brings them together and not in contact. No
feelings are interchanged, or sorrows or joys or hopes com-
municated. Unpreceded by inquiry or advice, command
and denunciation follow the roll call of the day." So Landor
wrote in 1836. In the forties there was a change of attitude,
due no doubt in part to the developments described in
a former chapter, when Nonconformists and Churchmen
alike threw themselves into two great public agitations on the side of the poor. Maurice and Kingsley were
creating a new conscience in the Christian Socialist
movement. The High Church Review, the *British
Critic*, was striking a new note in its comments on social
conditions. "The poor," it wrote, "have been deprived
of their games, their amusements, and their mirth. An
inventive age has multiplied to excess the toys and
recreations of the wealthy; while the poor are not to be
won and beguiled from sensual indulgence, and are only
to be preached to and terrified with tracts and tread-
mills, sermons and six months' imprisonment, into an
austere and servile morality." Prince Lee, the new
Bishop of Manchester, supported the movement for a
Free Library, and Hook, the Vicar of Leeds, urged the
town to buy Woodhouse Moor. Hook converted a
Church that was disliked and despised, when he went to
Leeds in 1838, into a Church that commanded respect
and affection in all classes. In his early days the
Chartists ran a list of candidates at the meeting for elect-

ing churchwardens, and carried all of them. The Chartist churchwardens, thus thrust upon Hook, learnt to admire him, and they worked with him and not against him. Workmen helped to administer all his organizations, and to provide funds for his schemes. He had no difficulty in raising the money needed for his parishes, and Church rates were never imposed. Hook, of course, was an exceptional man, but there is evidence that the new spirit of responsibility was beginning to affect the life of the Church. The Convocation of Canterbury passed a resolution in 1854 recommending that clergymen should live together in poor districts "preaching, exhorting, visiting the sick and poor in their own homes, and superintending schools." *The Times,* then in the full ardour of its campaign against ecclesiastical abuses, of which Trollope gives a picture in *The Warden,* observed dryly on this scheme: "Nothing could be more reasonable than these remarks, nor have we anything to add except that in reading them we appear to be reading the description of a collegiate or cathedral establishment engaged in its proper duties." At least the Church had travelled some way from the atmosphere in which Harcourt, the Archbishop of York from 1807 to 1847, had looked upon his duties. The story is told of him that when he was asked to hold a confirmation in the industrial districts of the West Riding, he replied that, if so, the confirmation must be held at Wakefield, for that was as far into the industrial West Riding as a gentleman could be expected to go.

A similar change is to be seen in the history of education. In the early years of the century the chief obstacle to popular education was the fear that it would be a social danger, imperilling the structure of society. In 1817 a Wesleyan Sunday-school in Bradford had to defend itself against critics who argued that "education would make the lower orders of society less disposed to submit to the constituted authorities and to act in a subordinate capacity." This was a widespread senti-

ment. In the forties there were fierce dissensions over
education, but the issue that divided the contending
parties was not whether children should be educated or
left ignorant, but whether they should be educated to be
Churchmen or to be Nonconformists. This controversy
was a serious obstacle to educational progress, but it did
not reflect the view so common at one time that the
children of the poor should not be educated at all. That
view still survived, no doubt, but no responsible man
would have defended it in public. Peel, speaking in
1847, said that the obstacle had passed away.

Another sign and result of the change of outlook was
the campaign for public museums and libraries. There
were libraries connected with Mechanics' Institutions,
and some millowners, like the Ashtons, the Strutts, the
Marshalls, and the Gregs, had established libraries for
their workpeople in early days. In the forties the practice
spread, and there are several references in the *Leeds
Intelligencer* and other papers to mills that provided
libraries and playgrounds. Peter Ainsworth and John
Bright had libraries for their workpeople. But there
were no public free libraries when Ewart, who occupies
in this crusade the place of honour that Brougham holds
in the crusade for adult education, began his campaign
in 1845. He proposed (March 6) that town councils
should be allowed to impose a rate to establish museums
of art, and he pointed out that with railway transport it
would be easy to send casts from town to town. The
debate showed how much this kind of provision was
needed, and how stiff were the obstacles. The fear of
allowing towns to spend public money was so strong that
the Bill was only allowed to pass when its operation had
been limited to towns with 10,000 inhabitants. The rate
sanctioned was $\frac{1}{2}d.$, and the charge for admission was
not to be more than 1d. The demand that museums
should be open on Sundays was rejected. In 1850 Ewart
introduced a new Bill to enable town councils to establish public libraries and museums. He proposed to

abolish the restriction of the existing Act to towns with
10,000 inhabitants, and to make admissions free. There
was strong opposition on the ground of extravagance,
led by Sibthorp. Brotherton, Bright, and W. J. Fox
supported Ewart, and in the division Cobden, Hume,
and Sir George Grey voted for the Bill, Disraeli and
Lord John Manners voting against. In the end Ewart
had to accept a compromise by which the Act was not
to be adopted by any town, unless two-thirds of the ratepayers had given their consent. No money might be
spent on buying books.

There were serious handicaps, but the movement
spread. Warrington and Salford had started small collec-
tions of books under the 1845 Museums Act; Manchester
was the first town to open a public library (in 1852)
under the new Act; Bolton and Liverpool followed in
1853; Sheffield, St. Helens, Birkenhead, and Preston
before 1860. In Manchester a committee of working men
was formed to collect a fund for buying books, and £800
was raised by 20,000 subscribers of the working classes
for this object, the total sum subscribed being over
£10,000.

The progress of the movement for public parks was
another sign of the same spirit. Far-sighted men like
R. A. Slaney had seen from the first how much town life
must suffer from the lack of open spaces (see p. 75).
The energetic James Silk Buckingham, better known as
a temperance reformer, who had started life as a sailor
and had been expelled from India for exposing abuses,
took up the cause during the five years in which he was
Member of Parliament for Sheffield. For three years in
succession he introduced Bills to "facilitate the formation of and establishment of Public Walks, Playgrounds,
Baths and Places of Healthy Recreation and Amusement." Buckingham was curiously sanguine when he
introduced his first Public Walks Bill, together with a
kindred Bill for providing Literary and Scientific Insti-
tutes and Museums. He expected, he said, no objection,

and declared that "in the course of a very few years, if
these Bills should pass into law, we shall see as many
public walks, gardens, and pleasure grounds in the
neighbourhood of all our towns, as are now to be found
on the Continent of Europe." But apathy proved as
effective as regular opposition. If one of his Bills
managed to reach the Report stage, consideration of the
Report was deferred again and again, and the session
came to an end without further progress. Some slight
notice was taken of the question in 1841, when the
Whigs made a grant of £10,000 for encouraging the provision of public walks and parks, but it was not till 1847
that local authorities were allowed to use the rates for
making a public park without obtaining a special Act.
The Towns Improvement Clauses Act contained this
provision, and it was incorporated in the Public Health
Act next year.

The earliest park seems to have been Preston Moor
Park, which the Corporation laid out in 1833–35.
Joseph Strutt's famous gift to Derby of the "Arboretum"
was made about 1840, costing him £10,000. There were
eleven acres of it "tastefully laid out in grass intersected
by broad gravel walks, and planted with a great variety
of trees, shrubs, and flowers botanically arranged." The
public were admitted free on Sundays, except during
service time, and on Wednesdays; on other days the
charge was 6d. In 1845 it was said to be much fre-
quented and to have "already produced a perceptible
effect in improving the appearance and demeanour of
the working classes, and it has doubtless conferred an
equal benefit upon their health." In 1843 Birkenhead
obtained a local Act setting aside 70 acres for recreation.
There was an active movement in Manchester in the
forties, and from private subscriptions and a grant of
£3,000 from the Government (out of the £10,000 voted),
three parks were bought, Peel's Park in Salford, and
Philips' and Queen's Park in Manchester, at a cost of
about £25,000. In 1855 Leeds bought Woodhouse Moor.

and Rochdale, Stockport, Blackburn, and Halifax all obtained parks in the fifties.

If we study the local history of the new towns, we find that private benefactions for public amenities became much more common in the forties and fifties. In this respect a change came over social life. One reason for the melancholy condition of the English manufacturing town was the tradition of private luxury which had become so powerful in the eighteenth century. Bishop Berkeley, writing in 1721, had dwelt on the strong contrast between ancient Greece and eighteenth-century England in this respect. Private splendour was as much a mark of the early industrial age as public meanness; the elegance of the great house as the gloom of the new town. The great house symbolized the pride the great lord took in his place in the national life. The mansion, with its libraries, galleries, parks, reflected the atmosphere of authority, of history, of taste and manners, of a life active, spacious, and delightful. A German observer noticed that Englishmen made more of their country house than of their town house. Now this attractive country life, with its beauty, culture, pleasure, and state, was open to all who made their way into the aristocracy, to the men whom success in business, their own or their father's, brought into this world. The governing class drew into its orbit almost all those who acquired wealth, setting the standard, mode, and plan of life. Hence the wealth of the early Industrial Revolution, if it was not invested, was largely used for creating new territorial families with mansions and estates in the country. The movement for parks and libraries first taught the English manufacturer and merchant to take a large view and to use their wealth in the spirit of the rich citizens of the Roman Empire.

Another sign of the times was the introduction of the Saturday half-holiday for clerks and the agitation for the earlier closing of shops. In 1844 the Manchester merchants decided to make Saturday a half-holiday for

all their employees, and this event was celebrated by a
soirée in the Town Hall. But the most striking and important manifestation of the new spirit was the success
of the Ten Hours Bill. The Bill won its way against the
prestige and power of the most experienced statesman
in public life. Peel, like Cobden, believed that to pass
the Ten Hours Bill was to invite industrial disaster.
Nobody who heard his speeches could think the danger
illusory. He enjoyed greater credit than any other man
in public life. He had been familiar from childhood with
industrial problems; he had extricated the finances of the
nation from the muddle left to him by his predecessors;
he had taken part in the reform of the factories; he had
shown on the income tax that he had larger views than
the capitalists, and on the Corn Laws that he had larger
views than the landlords; his skill and courage were unrivalled among men who had taken part in government;
of all debaters, free alike from Bright's bitterness and
Brougham's pedantry, he was the most persuasive,
giving invariably the impression that he was anxious to
answer a formidable argument rather than to evade it.
When he told his countrymen that the Ten Hours Bill
was a public danger, no man of sense thought that he
was saying what he did not believe, or that he believed
what he was saying for frivolous reasons.

The House of Commons in 1847 decided to take the
risk that Peel thought so menacing. And for what? To
banish from English life a terrible formula, the phrase
so long remembered in the mills of Lancashire, that the
workman's life was eating, drinking, working, and
sleeping. It was believed by the opponents of the Ten
Hours Bill that this melancholy formula drove the
wheels of Lancashire's industries and gave the English
people their proud place in the world. The English
people decided that they would risk the loss of that
position rather than let that formula oppress their
civilization any longer. It was a momentous choice, and
the future of England turned on the answer. If this

formula was to continue to rule her life, the English town could not hope to escape from the gloom that darkened the thirties. "Schools and libraries are of small use without time to study," so ran the Manifesto of the Short Time Central Committee in 1844. "Parks are well for those only who can have time to perambulate them, and baths are of little use to such dirty people as do not leave work till eight o'clock at night. We protest that it is a mere burlesque upon philanthropy to make provision for these benefits with a continuance of twelve hours' labour and fifteen hours' occupation for every manufacturing operative above thirteen years of age." Every step taken towards civilizing town life meant only another contrast between rich and poor, if the workman was to be shut up in the mill, while the well-to-do enjoyed themselves in the park and the library. The Ten Hours Act was in this sense the most important event in the first half of the century. The English people were trying to create a larger and more generous life for the English town. The Ten Hours Act meant that the workman was not to be shut out of it.

We get some idea of the difference that the new amenities made if we turn to the evidence given before the Committee on Public-Houses (1852–54). A Rational Recreation Association had been started at Leeds; popular concerts were given at the Town Hall, and the Botanical Gardens had now been thrown open on Sundays. Drunkenness had decreased and manners improved. At Manchester the parks were crowded on Sundays, and the Zoological Gardens were well attended by persons who before had spent Sunday dog-fighting or playing at pitch-and-toss in the beer-houses. At Liverpool, steamers took crowds across the river on Sundays, and Sunday had become less drunken. The Committee, reporting on such evidence, remarked: "Your Committee cannot conclude this portion of their Report without calling attention to the fact of how few places of rational enjoyment are open to the great masses of the population on Sunday, which serve as a counter-attraction to the public-house. They have it in evidence that wherever such opportunities have been provided, they have been eagerly seized upon, and have led to the decrease of intemperance."

A chapter of local history given to the first Conference of the National Association for the Promotion of Social Science in 1857 showed what could be done by such improvements to draw one of the new industrial towns out of its morass. A speaker who had taken an active part in public work at Macclesfield explained that in the year 1847–48 the death-rate in that town was 42 per thousand, and that one undrained district of seven streets was responsible for this high rate, as well as for the crime of the town. The Public Health Act was adopted and this district was cleansed and reformed, with the result that the death-rate had fallen to 26 per thousand. These improvements were followed by others. Baths and washhouses were installed, and a public park bought in which as many as 40 cricket matches were sometimes played on a single Saturday afternoon when the mills closed. This park was filled every evening in the summer. The opening of the park had been followed by a remarkable decrease of crime.

Wordsworth, describing mediæval society, made towns the nurseries of civilized custom:

> "Around those Churches, gathered Towns
> Safe from the feudal Castle's haughty frowns;
> Peaceful abodes, where Justice might uphold
> Her scales with even hand, and culture mould
> The heart to pity."

As he looked at the life of his own age, he gave the town a very different character:

> "there indeed
> Love cannot be nor does it thrive with ease
> Among the close and overcrowded haunts
> Of cities, where the human heart is sick
> And the eye feeds it not and cannot feed."

Culture was taught to mould the heart to pity, and light and happiness were brought into the disconsolate life of these overcrowded haunts by the efforts of men and women, such as this citizen of Macclesfield, whose influence on their civilization was as important as that of the statesmen who struggled over the Corn Laws. But in comparison they are as little known to fame as the monk whose patient labour saved for the world the Histories of Tacitus.

CHAPTER XIV

CONCLUSION

"Hitherto it is questionable if all the mechanical inventions yet made have lightened the day's toil of any human being. They have enabled a greater population to live the same life of drudgery and imprisonment, and an increased number of manufacturers and others to make fortunes. They have increased the comforts of the middle classes. But they have not yet begun to effect those great changes in human destiny, which it is in their nature and in their futurity to accomplish."—Mill, Political Economy (*Third Edition*), *ii.* 332.

THE English people began, a century ago, to make a new society out of a rapidly growing population which had left peasant life and peasant surroundings to find work in the new industries and homes in the new towns. This book is a survey of their first experiment in that task: an experiment guided by a particular view of human nature. The rulers of these towns believed that a society of men getting on, trying to get on, thinking always of getting on, and sacrificing everything to getting on, would be a happy and stable society.

The virtues on which this view insisted, industry, sobriety, thrift, self-control, have a special value in times of excitement and change. It is not perhaps surprising that they seemed to make up the whole of good citizenship to men living close to the England that Hogarth painted. There was still a good deal of that England left in spite of Wesley's heroic exertions. But in concentrating on these virtues the rulers of this society put on one side pursuits and enjoyments that have interested man at different times of his history, and helped to develop his taste, his imagination, and his

239

character. Beauty was given no place in work or play, in culture or religion. Nobody can read the description of Coventry in the fifteenth century, with its full life of festival and play, given by Conrad Gill in his *Studies in Midland History*, and then turn to Faucher's description of Manchester, without seeing how complete was the breach between the city life of that time and the city life of the Industrial Revolution.

Mill, criticizing this social life, contrasted it with the life of the Continent, and said that the British insensibility to art as a social influence was one reason why England and the Continent could not understand each other. He traced it to three sources: the money-getting spirit which regarded as a loss of time everything that did not conduce directly to its own end, religious Puritanism, which looked on feeling as a snare, and the imperfect and misleading psychology of Bentham which, in its simplifying analysis of human motives, left out of account the love of beauty. The first two influences had chiefly shaped the British character since Stuart times; the third was the most powerful influence on the mind of the age. Mill wrote on this third cause with all the more feeling because he was himself a victim of an upbringing misdirected by its influence. In his *Autobiography* he described how, having had a very thorough but purely intellectual education beginning at the age of three, in which feeling was entirely disregarded, he had what we should call a nervous breakdown at the age of twenty. He found peace and relief in the study of Wordsworth.

No educated man will question the immense benefits that Bentham conferred on the English people. Lord Acton, speaking of the intuition that started him on the task of disentangling the injustices of the law, said that "the day on which that gleam lighted up the clear hard mind of Jeremy Bentham is memorable in the political calendar beyond the entire administration of many statesmen." Mill said of him that he found the philo-

sophy of law a chaos, and left it a science, and that he
held an indisputable place among the intellectual benefactors of mankind. But it happens that those deficiencies
on which Mill dwelt in his description have a close bearing
on the social life of the new towns. For his misleading
view of human nature led Bentham to construct a world
which Mill described as a collection of persons each
pursuing his separate interest or pleasure, in which the
law, religion, and public opinion, imposing their several
sanctions, serve to prevent more jostling than is
unavoidable.

This conception, limited enough in its original form,
was not likely to become less limited in the hands of the
men who applied it to the new settlements calling for
guidance and leadership. The energetic man of business,
when told that the best way for him to help the poor of
Manchester and Leeds was to make haste to get richer,
was not likely to ask himself whether so simple and
encouraging a gospel contained the whole truth about
something so complicated as a human society, to throw
his mind back over history, to recall what had been said
on such subjects by Plato or Cicero or St. Augustine or
Shakespeare. Nor did it get any less limited in the hands
of leaders of morals and manners, who thought that a
workman spending a quiet Sunday morning in the
public park, when he ought to be in chapel in a black
coat, was a spectacle so offensive to God that it would
bring down on the nation the Divine displeasure.

This philosophy, applied to industry and social life, provoked two agitations, an agitation in the world of literature and an agitation in the world of politics. All that
Bentham had forgotten crowded into the pages of Shelley
and Wordsworth, Coleridge and Southey, Carlyle and
Dickens, Mill and Maurice, Peacock and Disraeli: pages
gentle or stern, lucid or confused, pensive or ironical,
playing with fancies or thundering with passion. To
understand why the Chartist was a figure in history more
complex than a man demanding a higher wage, or

resenting a particular grievance, we must remember how
deeply men and women may be stirred by emotions
which they can neither describe nor interpret. The inco-
herent anger of Manchester and Leeds reflected what
those writers had discerned, however unsuccessful they
might be in devising remedies: the sickness of a society
in which essential instincts were left unsatisfied. The
ordinary man would not have put his case as it was put
by Wordsworth, or Maurice, or Carlyle, but the error
in the ruling philosophy of the time that provoked those
writers was the injustice in life that provoked those
rebels. Men and women knew that they were the victims
of wrong, and that something was false in their world.

We are thus brought back to the comparison with
which we started. In all ages the service of man's needs
has occupied great numbers of men and women in hard,
distasteful, and monotonous toil. The ancient world
offered one consolation for that toil, the world of the
Industrial Revolution another. The ancient world sought
to make that lot tolerable by the play of life and laughter
and beauty in its cities. The poor man, sharing the
delights of admiration and the comforts of fellowship,
could imagine that drudgery was only part of his life,
for when the city gave its mind to religion or festival, he
stood beside his neighbour, a man among men, lost like
his fellows in contemplation or enjoyment. The new age
offered the prizes of wealth and rank to those who ex-
celled in that toil, but it treated delights, that had once
made the hardships of common life less rigid and
monotonous, as the rewards of rare success. The arts,
instead of helping the complaining and miserable to
forget themselves and their wrongs, were employed to
give a new lustre to good fortune, to declare the glory
of sudden wealth. Leisure was the exclusive privilege of
those for whom work was interesting, giving to those
engaged in it a bracing sense of power.

Now ancient civilization, at its best, was disfigured by
injustices that would have outraged the conscience of

the age of Bentham, and by cruelties that would have revolted its sense of pity. The critic of the Roman Empire as an experiment in making a stable and contented society might have pointed to Christianity and similar religions, spreading in the great towns the voice of a misery that was bitterly resented. He might have pointed, too, to the efforts of philosophers to satisfy their consciences by a more direct encounter with those facts of poverty and slavery which civilization sought to mask beneath its smiling amenities; some explaining them in terms of science, others denying that such hardship could touch the soul, others, again, taking the heaviest burdens on their own backs to prove how light such burdens were when carried by men who had learnt the difference between true happiness and false. He could thus have shown that the failures of these efforts were as striking as their successes. Yet there was a truth behind those efforts that this new age, rich as it was in knowledge where ancient civilization was ignorant, had still to grasp.

It is obvious that for the majority of human beings a great part of life is occupied with the hard struggle for material security, or material success. The rulers of Manchester or Leeds believed that man could find his happiness in that struggle, clothing it with ambition or piety, giving the look of romance to its dramatic episodes, and making success or failure in that struggle the mark of success or failure in the whole art of life. They held that you could treat the desire to grow rich as the object of universal ambition, and that if the path to its attainment was thrown open, the poor man plodding at his tedious task might dream of his future with all the happiness that Fielding attributed to the young barrister dreaming of the Woolsack. Such a plan of life assumed that this struggle called out all man's faculties, that it symbolized somehow the whole of his history, and that it left unemployed and unsatisfied no important element in his nature.

No man can reflect on his own experience without seeing that there is a kind of happiness which is outside that struggle. The happiness that comes to a man when he follows a great play or listens to great music, when he stands beneath a noble building or looks out over a golden landscape, bears no relation to his own ambitions or his own success. The Greeks who could enjoy the plays of Æschylus and Euripides had been taught to look on the drama as part of their religious experience, lifting the curtain from ideas too large for daily life. Bradley makes a comment on Wordsworth and Hegel in his *Essay on English Poetry* ("A Miscellany") which helps to illustrate the argument of these pages. He says of their philosophy that "the mind of man is no property of his; indeed, we might say, his private share in it consists of its limitations, while its greatness is all derived." In this sense the arts, like religion, enable a man to escape from his limitations into the peace and beauty that belong to a universal mind; to re-enter the life of a world that lived before him and will live after him. The man who can never so escape is like the man described by Lucretius (III, 1060) who dashes from his home to the country, and from the country to his home, restless and weary, a sick man who knows not the cause of his complaint.

To make a society out of men who are sick is to make a sick society. Between the spirit of Athens and that of a goldfield, between a number of persons whose bond of union is their enjoyment of art, religion, beauty, and amusement, and the same number of persons whose bond of union is that each of them hopes to become a rich man, there is a difference that affects the depths and not merely the surface of social life. Man who started on his upward path, led by wonder, learning from nature, blending toil with ceremony, with religion, with dance and play, cannot be shut inside the narrow circle devised by the economists without suffering mortal strain. That is why, when society is sick from this cause, humanists, who are concerned for man's spiritual interest, have attacked, not merely the abuses of their age, but its fundamental philosophy. That is why Cicero, looking at Rome's age of plunder, said that the worst of all constitutions was that in which the richest men were counted the best. That is why Mill, looking at the age of the Industrial Revolution, declared that "the best state for human nature is that in which, while no one is poor, no one desires to be richer, nor has any reason to fear being thrust back, by the efforts of others to push themselves forward."

For the humanists saw that the progress of man has been due to his capacity for disinterested enjoyment and generous pleasure, and that he has succeeded in making societies, just because he could find some other bond between men than the bonds understood by Cato. The pursuit of knowledge and ideas, the search for beauty and feeling in culture and religion, the emotions of pride and pity excited by a common literature and history, these have spread the deeper spirit of fellowship. The ties which unite societies, crossing the barriers of class, of race, and of time, are created by the sympathies that have civilized the habits and the mind of man. "So that if the invention of the ship," wrote Bacon, in a famous passage, "was thought so noble, which carrieth riches and commodities from place to place, and consociateth the most remote regions in participation of their fruits, how much more are letters to be magnified, which as ships pass through the vast seas of time, and make ages so distant to participate of the wisdom, illuminations, and inventions, the one of the other?"

Bridges, describing the birth of man's mind from his response to the beauty of nature, drew a picture of the wolf hunting all his life after nightfall, under starlit skies, without the first inklings of wonder. Yet even the wolf, as he steals across the silence of Mount Olympus, may turn to gaze on the vast peace that lies over the enchanted world described in *Endymion*, the world of bird and beast, of sea and mountain, sleeping in the silver moonlight. The men and women who now lived in blind streets had lived, themselves or their fathers, beneath the open spaces of heaven. In the high moments of his history man has answered the beauty of nature with the beauty of cities, but for these exiles the dreams of mind and hand were as faint and distant as the mountains and the forests whence those dreams had come. No public grace adorned their towns; religion was too often a stern and selfish fantasy; music and painting were strangers, at home among the elegant rich, but doubtful of their welcome in this raw confusion; ships brought the riches of the East across the Indian Ocean, but those other ships which "pass through the vast seas of time" never spread their splendid sails. Science herself, the goddess of the age, kept her gifts for the fortunate. For though man's power and knowledge had made a new world since Odysseus fretted for his home in Calypso's cavern, the spinner, guiding the myriad wheels that clothed the distant East, was condemned to spend his life longing, like Homer's ploughman, for the hour of sunset and supper. But the spirit of wonder which had created art and religion, music and letters, gardens and playing-fields, still lingered in the toiling men and women who were shut within these sullen streets. That spirit could not live at peace in treadmill cities where the daylight never broke upon the beauty and the wisdom of the world.

INDEX